Our Children Are Alcoholics

Coping with Children Who Have Addictions

"Sally and Dave's book comes from real life and helps guide parents, often ignored or blamed in the past, toward a direction of their own health and growth."

Robert Landeen, MD
Addictionologist and
Assistant Professor of Clinical Psychiatry
Stanford University

Sally B and David B

Sally and David B.

Learn how to find serenity in the midst of chaos

The authors wish to remain anonymous in accordance with the tried and true tradition of Al-Anon, whose public relations policy is one of always maintaining personal anonymity at the level of press, radio, TV, and film. In addition, Al-Anon members are careful to guard the anonymity of all AA members. *Therefore, the authors ask representatives of the media to respect the authors' use of their first names and last initial only.* In this way the authors protect the anonymity of their children and themselves.

Note: The names, locations, and types of work of all the children and all the other parents in every story have been changed completely.

Book Team
Publisher: Sandra J. Hirstein
Managing Editor: Mary Jo Graham
Assistant Editor: Sharon K. Cruse
Cover Design: Mike Meyer
Interior Design: Veronica Burnett
Composition: Kymberly Schmitt

Copyright © 1997 by Islewest Publishing,
a division of Carlisle Communications, Inc.
4242 Chavenelle Drive, Dubuque, IA 52002.
800-557-9867   www.Islewest.com
All rights reserved.

Manufactured in the United States of America.

Library of Congress Catalog Card Number: 97-070959

ISBN 1-888461-02-0

A Letter From an Alcoholic

To my Family—

I am an alcoholic. I need your help.

Don't lecture, blame or scold me. You wouldn't be angry at me for having TB or diabetes. Alcoholism is a disease, too.

Don't pour out my liquor; it's just a waste because I can always find ways of getting more.

Don't let me provoke your anger. If you attack me verbally or physically, you will only confirm my bad opinion of myself. I hate myself enough already.

Don't let your love and anxiety for me lead you into doing what I ought to do for myself. If you assume my responsibilities, you make my failure to assume them permanent. My sense of guilt will be increased, and you will feel resentful.

Don't accept my promises. I'll promise anything to get off the hook. But the nature of my illness prevents me from keeping my promises, even though I mean them at the time.

Don't make empty threats. Once you have made a decision, stick to it.

Don't believe everything I tell you; it may be a lie. Denial of reality is a symptom of my illness. Moreover, I'm likely to lose respect for those I can fool too easily.

Don't let me take advantage of you or exploit you in any way. Love cannot exist for long without the dimension of justice.

Don't cover up for me or try in any way to spare me the consequences of my drinking. Don't lie for me, pay my bills, or meet my obligations. It may avert or reduce the very crisis that would prompt me to seek help. I can continue to deny that I have a drinking problem as long as you provide an automatic escape from the consequences of my drinking.

Above all, *do* learn all you can about alcoholism and your role in relation to me. Go to open AA meetings when you can. Attend Al-Anon meetings regularly, read the literature and keep in touch with Al-Anon members. They're the people who can help you see the whole situation clearly.

I love you.
Your alcoholic

From 3 *Views of Al-Anon*, copyright © 1970, 1971 by Al-Anon Family Group Headquarters, Inc. Reprinted by permission of Al Anon Family Group Headquarters, Inc. Based on material which appears in *Guide for the Family of the Alcoholic*, Reverend Joseph L. Kellerman, Al-Anon Family Group Headquarters, Inc., Virginia Beach, Va.

Acknowledgements

This book has been a labor of love. It would never have been written without the devoted education we have received over nearly twenty years from the fellowships of Alcoholics Anonymous and Al-Anon. Many of you are noted anonymously throughout the book.

We are very grateful to the parents who so courageously tell their stories here. Like angelic messengers, they are passing on their experience, strength, and hope in the unselfish desire to help other suffering parents take heart.

Many wonderful friends and colleagues who must remain anonymous have encouraged and critiqued our efforts. We thank you all.

Special thanks are due several persons. Chaplain Ann Marie Wood, RN, DMin suggested numerous detailed improvements that greatly strengthened the manuscript before our publisher took it in hand.

The Rev. Paul and Jan Chaffee introduced us to the Marin Small Publishers association, where we have been learning about writing and publishing.

Carol Ormandy introduced us to the poetry of Wendell Berry, and suggested his poem which begins our story.

Stephanie Brown, Ph.D., impressed on us from her own wide experience as a researcher and author the challenges and pitfalls of maintaining anonymity whenever the written word enters the public domain.

Robert H. Landeen, M.D., and Richard B. Seymour, M.A., read part II for accuracy and made several valuable suggestions, as did Mary Frances Rimerman, M.A. Their professional expertise has been indispensable. Any remaining inaccuracies are the authors'.

Many thanks to Betsy Blosser, Ph.D., and Kathy McKennan, R.N., for referrals to useful videos.

We cannot adequately thank Islewest and our editor, Mary Jo Graham, for their faith in this book and the vision to see it through.

Finally, we bless our four children for believing in us, supporting us, critiquing each part of our family's story, and contributing their own sections. They are truly our heroes.

Contents

Preface

The purpose of this book is to provide relief and reassurance for beleaguered parents of alcoholics and addicts. The parents in these pages describe how they have found serenity even in the midst of chaos, and regardless of whether their addicted children are clean and sober. We know from experience that recovery for parents is a long process, with many setbacks, but there is much hope for the parents. However, we cannot tell anyone how to "get your child clean and sober." That is because an addict's recovery is not contingent on what parents or others do or don't do, although we may play a role if we have accurate information about the disease, and if we learn how we might react differently.

Ten or twelve years ago Sally was looking for published material that would help enlarge an understanding of the role of parents of alcoholic children. Surprisingly, there wasn't any that she could find, though bookstores carried a wealth of related information on addiction, on adult children of alcoholics, on codependency, and so on. A handful of brief introductory pamphlets and booklets (some now out of print) on parents of adolescent alcoholics and addicts were available through a few limited outlets specializing in addiction literature, mostly mail order. But there was nothing readily accessible to the general public, and nothing about adult children.

On an impulse Sally made a quick outline of what she would want in such a book. The content would consist mostly of stories of parents' actual experiences, for we had learned those not only gave us hope, they were the most meaningful way to learn what worked and what didn't. Then in the press of demands on her time, she forgot about it. She didn't discard the outline, however. It languished at the bottom of the basket on her desk. Every few months, when she cleaned out the basket, she would rediscover the outline and once again search the bookstores in hopes of finding that someone had written about parents of alcoholics.

Meanwhile, people who knew our family story suggested from time to time that we should write it down to share with a general public that undoubtedly had many suffering, confused parents of alcoholic and addicted children. Someone also once commented that in retrospect our family has been like a row of dominoes, one after the other falling into recovery (though it took sixteen years all told, and with no guarantees of permanence, that being the nature of addictive disease). Such wholesale recovery may be unusual, and as parents we claim little credit. A Power beyond our own was truly at work when we finally stepped out of the way.

Probably nothing more than a possible outline would have materialized, however, if one day Sally hadn't mentioned to our youngest daughter the latent urge to collect the stories of parents of alcoholics. This daughter had had some recent experience with writing, editing, and publishing. She suggested that before we got too involved, it would be a good idea to write our own family's story, and send it to selected agents and publishers with a proposed outline. Thus began the evolution of this book.

We hope our story, and those of many others, will help parents like us find the hope, the tools, and the support we've found—things we parents urgently need for the long haul in confronting the scourge of addictive disease in our children. You are not alone.

Sally and David B.

Introduction

On airplanes we are told that if the cabin pressure drops, oxygen masks will automatically descend. If a child is seated next to us, we are to put on our own mask first, then the child's. Likewise, we parents who are frantically trying to save our children from the consequences of addictive disease, must take steps to save ourselves. We can be more help to everyone around us if we're willing to put on our own oxygen masks.

Unfortunately, the airplane oxygen mask metaphor then breaks down, for we cannot predict that a child will accept the oxygen of recovery, or maintain recovery thereafter. There is no cause and effect relationship between a parent's getting help for living with an addicted child, and that child's starting recovery. Some children get well, some don't.

Sadly, yet realistically, a parent may be the last person from whom an addicted child will ever agree to receive that oxygen. However, regardless of what our children do or don't do, we parents can choose our own restoration to an abundant life not only worth living, but full of serenity and joy. Anxiety and fear can essentially vanish for us. Sounds impossible, doesn't it?

When we first learned in 1978 that one of our daughters was an alcoholic, we were in shock and frantic with worry. We're very grateful that eventually we took the advice of friends and professional counselors, and began attending Al-Anon, the successful, experienced self-help recovery groups for friends and families of alcoholics (for more about Al-Anon, see the appendix). As our other three children also succumbed to this dreadful disease, we continued our participation in the recovery groups in order to preserve our own sanity and balance.

The single most important common denominator of parental recovery is almost always found through being in a group that both understands what the parent is experiencing and also provides the tools to adjust to a saner way of living. This is true of the brave parents who share their stories in the following pages. All of them have sought recovery in a group that meets their needs. Often beaten to their knees by extreme worry and a foreboding sense of terrible powerlessness over what's happening to their addicted children of whatever age, these parents have finally admitted they need the help of others. Gasping, they've grabbed for the oxygen and found life again.

The main reason most people, parents included, initially seek help for coping with someone who has addictive disease is because they passionately want to find out how to cure the alcoholic or addict in their lives—how to stop the drinking and using. They're sure that then they can relax and feel better. Instead they discover they have the power to change only themselves. It's an awful shock at first. Parents may feel cheated. Those accustomed to degrees of influence over their children are especially bewildered and often resentful.

What can be predicted for parents who get help is a significant reduction in tension and an improvement in their own attitudes and behaviors. As people learn about addictive disease, they come to understand and welcome the limitations of a powerlessness that paradoxically produces strength and release, not weakness and constraint. Painful experience further demonstrates that, lacking informed support and reinforcement from others, it is extremely difficult to make the necessary changes just on one's own.

The parents in this book tell in their own words how they found their way to health and serenity in the midst of turmoil. Many of them are in Al-Anon (a 12-step program for families and friends of alcoholics), the self-help companion to Alcoholics Anonymous (see glossary for both organizations). Others have found recovery through their churches, therapy groups, or additional kinds of support settings. Because we have learned that it is possible to live a happy and fulfilling life regardless of whether one's child has stopped drinking or using, our main criterion in selecting stories was that a parent be in some degree of recovery.

Each story describes what it was like for that parent, what happened, and what it's like now. The plot line in all the stories is more common than might be thought, although the details will differ from family to family, and even from parent to parent in the same family. If you have an addicted child, we believe you will see yourself or your situation in someone's story. To protect everyone's anonymity, we have used pseudonyms throughout, and have disguised residential locations and places of work.

Part I. Four separate accounts describing our experience with addictive disease in our four adult children. Like this introduction, it is written mostly in Sally's voice, but Dave has been both editor and contributor.

Every one of our four children presented us with very different problems. We constantly felt we were having to start from scratch. With each child we learned something new, basic, and extremely important in our cumulative understanding of addictive disease. Following each of our family's four stories, that adult child will briefly describe what was going on with him/her, and how Dave and I were viewed as parents.

Part II. Discusses addictive disease, together with its known effects on families, friends, and coworkers.

Part III. Presents numerous stories by many parents of addicted children, illustrating a variety of family constellations. The children range in age from young teenagers to middle-aged adults.

Part IV. Contains resources: bibliography, community resources, audiovisuals, catalogs, and a glossary.

In popular understanding, alcoholism and addiction are often considered to be separate conditions. They are, however, merely two different names for a single affliction, now known accurately as addictive disease. Whenever *alcoholism* or *addiction* is used in this book, the term should be understood as referring to the broader meaning, *addictive disease*. The addictive substances encompass alcohol, nicotine, street drugs, some prescription drugs, and some foods, including caffeine and sugar.

The standard unofficial figure for the incidence of adult alcoholism alone in the population of the United States is 10 percent, or about 22,500,000 persons. Considering that each alcoholic has a mother and father, the majority of them probably still living in these times of extended age spans, it is surprising that parents are not better represented in recovery groups. There are many reasons. Here are the most common ones. We have known them all:

Denial.   Probably the single most important reason that parents fail to get help, denial usually takes two forms: (1) denial that addiction may be the primary cause of most, if not all, of their child's problems; and (2) denial that the parent needs help. "Why me? It's Jimmy (or Jane or Dick or Debbie) that needs the help. I'd be fine if he/she would just shape up and I didn't have all these worries!"

Shame. "I'm so ashamed of my child's behavior. I never brought my kid up to steal (drink, use, lie, etc.)!"

Resentment. "All he/she does is lie around and watch TV. Doesn't even try to get a job!"

Secrecy. "I mustn't let anyone know that my child is a drunk (addict, felon, etc.). What would my friends (my mother, the people at work, etc.) think?"

Guilt. "I feel so guilty for failing to raise my child properly. If only I'd been smarter (stricter, less strict, etc.)."

Delusions of power. "A parent is the best person to help one's child. Who else knows him or her better?"

Minimizing. "It's just an experimental phase all teenagers and young adults go through. I did it myself. He/she will grow out of it."

Excusing. "If it weren't for the stress of his/her job (marriage, relationship, school, etc.), he/she would be fine."

Blaming others. "If it weren't for those no-good 'friends', he/she would be fine."

Whatever the particular combination of parental ideas and attitudes, however, the basic feelings of parents for their children are universal regardless of socioeconomic, ethnic, and educational background. Our children never stop being our children. We hurt when our children hurt.

For us, Al-Anon and related 12-step programs became our lifeline. Al-Anon is primarily composed of spouses or partners of alcoholics/addicts, and of adult children of alcoholics. Not until the last few years have we begun to encounter more parents of alcoholics. Parents of alcoholics are still a distinct minority in the traditional recovery groups. However, in some parts of the country, recovery groups just for parents of alcoholics have sprung up.

Sometimes the parents we meet are young, with alcoholic teenagers. Or the parents may be in their sixties and occasionally seventies, with middle-aged alcoholic adult children. These older parents frequently have additional heartbreaking concerns for grandchildren being neglected or abused in the home of an alcoholic son or daughter.

Sometimes one or both parents of alcoholic children are recovering alcoholics themselves. This is truly a family disease. Someday a genetic basis may be identified. We believe this disease has an inheritable component. Besides alcohol and drugs, addictions to food and nicotine are present in our own immediate nuclear family. This constellation of addictions is also found in extended family members of our generation, in some of our children's cousins, and in our grandparents' generation. Several relatives have died of alcoholism, including Sally's brother. We observe that addictive disease is widespread in the generations of families we encounter in our recovery groups.

Occasionally, though, neither parent has any known family history of addiction. In these cases the disease seems to have surfaced unaccountably and mysteriously in an adult child. We're always amazed that these bewildered parental innocents find the Al-Anon recovery groups. The alcoholic parent may be quicker to recognize and accept the existence of addiction in the adult alcoholic child, but all parents fear the consequences and grieve for their children.

While the recovery groups have been indispensable teachers and guides for us, some of the issues related to being the parent of an alcoholic/addict are not generally recognized clearly or articulated well. This can be a lonely feeling at times, especially for newcomer parents who may not immediately connect their own stories with the universal themes in the stories of distraught spouses and adult children of alcoholics.

In addition, we've found that parents of alcoholic children do have some significant extra concerns.

For example, there are primary parental protective instincts to save a child's life, whether the child is four or forty. Fear that one's child could die from addiction severely affects the attitudes and behaviors of fed-up, frightened, befuddled parents. This elemental fear of a parent for one's child seems to exceed the very strong fears felt for addicted spouses/partners, or even that of children for their addicted parents.

Besides fear, there are parental feelings of shame, anger, and grief that a child can fall afoul of the law, disgrace a family's image, or not fulfill his or her potential. Many parents are baffled and mortified by what they perceive as unacceptable failures of morality, willpower, or self-control in their children. These parental responses are typical whether the parent is a true nonaddict, an unacknowledged addict, or a recovering addict, especially if the parents are living apparently upright, productive lives. There are powerful issues of parental control and expectations, even when the child is fully adult.

The problems are compounded when the parent is uninformed or misinformed about the disease of addiction, not realizing that tried-and-true principles of parenting—such as rescuing, scolding, threatening, or protecting the minor or adult child in trouble—won't work well in the case of addictive disease. Learning to let go, and "detach with love" from a suffering child goes against every normal parental instinct. Everything within us as parents screams that we can't possibly allow a beloved child to spiral down into certain disaster or death. Parents aren't supposed to back off. We're supposed to help. But addictive disease is a strange, paradoxical beast that requires turning upside down most of our notions of what it means to "help." The parental stories in this book repeatedly demonstrate that the best response to the afflicted person is often counterintuitive.

Every story describes a process of parental adaptation to addictive disease in an adult child or children. The focus is on the parent. Each story also ends with a snapshot in time, where the parent pauses with whatever is happening at that particular moment. A year from now, or five years, the story will be different. We need to remember the fluid nature of addictive disease and recovery in both parent and child.

Eventually, despite all your resistance, you may finally be propelled by these stories, as we and other parents have been, to seek relief from fear, despair, and demoralization; from that wild sense of life spinning out of control; and from anger, confusion, and often somatic symptoms in ourselves, such as physical exhaustion, insomnia, headaches, and stomach upsets. We urge you to set aside your pride, your shame, your fear of losing control, and let others who are walking your same path help you. Choose to live!

PART I
THE STORY
OF OUR FAMILY

TO MY CHILDREN,
FEARING FOR THEM

*Terrors are to come. The earth
is poisoned with narrow lives.
I think of you. What you will*

*live through, or perish by, eats
at my heart. What have I done? I
need better answers than there are*

*to the pain of coming to see
what was done in blindness,
loving what I cannot save. Nor,*

*your eyes, turning toward me,
can I wish your lives unmade
though the pain of them is on me.*

``To My Children, Fearing for Them" from OPENINGS copyright 1968 and renewed
1996 by Wendell Berry, reprinted by permission of Harcourt Brace & Company.

The Beginning

I married my college sweetheart toward the end of World War II. Dave became a successful electrical engineer, in at the birth and ensuing development of the computer revolution. He recently retired after fifty years of a fulfilling career.

For the first twenty years of marriage I was a fairly typical stay-at-home mom. We produced four baby-boomer children—a boy and three girls. I loved motherhood and adored our children, and would go to any lengths to nurture and protect them. We were a close, loving family, but I was definitely into benign dictatorship. That was a mother's role as I saw it, and I failed to recognize the need to back off and let go sufficiently once the children grew up.

Dave was very busy as his career advanced rapidly, but he made a decision when the children were small that he would not become an absentee father. His family would always come first. Except for frequent and sometimes extended travel periods, he was usually home for dinner and weekends, and rarely brought his work with him.

We were blessed with a solid decade of a very good marriage before I turned to alcohol after our last child was born. Until then, we rarely had any kind of liquor in the house. Our use of alcohol increased, and I rapidly developed into a full-blown alcoholic without any of us realizing what was happening. We thought that we were into the good life and being stylish. Both of us drank. Even as my drinking became out of control, I continued to function acceptably as a mother and a wife. Because the house was kept in order and meals were on the table, Dave believed all was well. Our children were bright and healthy. We appeared to be a typical upper-middle-class family.

Then our marriage began to have its problems. Still Dave was in strong denial that anything was seriously wrong. If he ever had a thought that alcohol was a contributing factor, he minimized it and tried to put it out of his mind. Today he says, "Undoubtedly my denial was related to pride in my family. I couldn't accept the fact that alcoholism was undermining the family and affecting my marriage."

After we'd been married about thirty years, Dave received some management training at work that included lectures by a man from the National Council on Alcoholism (now called the National Council on Alcoholism and Drug Dependence—NCADD—see glossary). This was his first exposure to factual information about alcoholism. He promptly applied his new knowledge to his work situation (for example, recognizing that his company's vice president was an alcoholic, dealing with a colleague who went on a binge just before an important report was due, and so on).

But his knowledge about alcoholism was limited to the workplace. On the home front, denial ruled. Dave's belief that nothing could be wrong with his family was so strong that he could not see, or refused to admit, what was happening to his wife. He would come home from work and observe that I was breathing strangely.

"Are you all right?" he would ask.

"Yes, I'm fine." That was all he wanted to hear.

Dave's denial applied to problems with our children as well. Both of us knew our teenagers were experimenting with marijuana, and we heard some sad stories about LSD and a few of their friends. Dave's main concern was that these drugs were illegal, not that they were addictive. Neither of us had a clue about what was really going on.

As the children entered school, I found exciting outside interests before my drinking interfered too greatly. I acquired a graduate degree in therapeutic recreation, followed by many years of consulting and college teaching in this field. These outwardly successful activities, however, masked the acceleration of my disease. Dave's blindness wasn't just a matter of denial on his part; I worked hard to hide the extent of my addiction.

Between Dave's denial and my dissembling, he didn't really believe I was an alcoholic until about three months after I stopped drinking, when he was startled to see a positive balance in the checkbook. He'd had no idea whatsoever how much alcohol I was buying—and consuming!

When I finally sought recovery in Alcoholics Anonymous (AA—see glossary) in August 1977, twenty-two years after starting to drink, Dave and I were temporarily living in Arlington, Virginia, next to Washington, D.C. He was relieved by my apparent return to health, and generally pleased and supportive.

In AA I learned that alcoholism is a disease, not a moral lapse or failure of willpower anymore than cancer and diabetes are. That scientific fact didn't excuse my behaviors while in the active stages of alcoholism, whether drunk at the time or not. I still had many amends to make. But the factual identification of addiction as a disease—characterized by an abnormal physiology and biochemistry that I didn't cause and couldn't control for long if I took an addictive substance—relieved me of a huge burden and reduced the stigma I felt. Dave and I are very grateful that we learned this lesson about addictive disease immediately, because it later saved us much misunderstanding and grief in relating to our addicted adult children. (See part 2 for a fuller description of addictive disease.)

We were a continent away from our now grown children, who lived and worked or went to school in the San Francisco Bay Area. Our youngest daughter, Rosie, was the only one married. Sarah had earned her bachelor of arts degree, but was driving a cab until she decided what to do next. Susan, our oldest daughter, also had her bachelor's degree, in art history, and was temping as a secretary. Our son, Andy, the eldest child, was starting his third year of college.

Sarah's Problem Begins to Surface

Our middle daughter, Sarah, was the first of our children to be identified with addictive disease. She was ill the longest and most acutely, and was the last to find recovery. So our learning and coping processes relative to her were the most time-consuming.

A few months after I got sober, Dave and I began to receive letters and phone calls from Sarah's brother and sisters, saying something was seriously wrong with her. They felt she needed psychiatric care because some of her behavior was so bizarre, such as pulling down the drapes in a trance-like state, or methodically opening and dumping jar after jar of spices on the floor one evening when she came to visit. Another time she called the San Francisco police and told them her older sister, Susan, was committing suicide. Imagine the consternation of both police and Susan, when the officers rudely awakened her from a peaceful, sound sleep.

I told new friends in AA what was happening back home in California. To my surprise they immediately asked, "Does she have a drinking problem?" Dave and I had no idea, but we quizzed our three concerned children. They were pretty sure that Sarah did not have a drinking problem. She had a beer once in a while, but so did they. They believed that their sister had a mental problem.

Dave and I were perplexed because we didn't know much at the time about mental illness, and little more about addictive disease. Even though I knew and accepted the fact that I was an alcoholic, and Dave had had that management training in alcoholism, we still had a hazy notion of "real" alcoholics as being skid-row bums. Somewhat tentatively, I decided to keep an open mind about the possibility of alcohol or drugs causing Sarah's irrational moods and actions. True to form, Dave was unconvinced that alcohol could explain her behavior.

In the meantime, we were rapidly gaining new information about alcoholism and addiction during my early months of recovery. People in AA told me how alcoholics and addicts could act "crazy." Many of my new friends thought they themselves were crazy before they got sober, never realizing the alcohol was making them that way. Indeed, before the proliferation of alcohol and drug treatment programs, alcoholics were routinely hospitalized in psychiatric wards. My recovering friends also said that when alcoholics stopped drinking, and their physical, mental, and emotional systems began to heal, most, if not all, of the insanity disappeared. Whatever mental problems remained could usually be effectively treated. It was our first experience in recognizing that alcoholism could often be accurately diagnosed by secondary behaviors like acting crazy. You didn't actually have to observe the person drinking to excess, or falling-down drunk.

I also learned that if this disease was not arrested, or was left untreated, the certain outcome was either a "wet brain" (irreversible insanity) or death. This was a frightening thought in relation to Sarah. She was a gifted student who had just graduated with honors from a prestigious college. What if she was an alcoholic and her brain was already permanently damaged?

Not long after we learned how concerned Sarah's siblings were about her, and when we'd barely started our own self-education in addictive disease, an unexpected nightmare began. One night, from deep in sleep I heard a loud insistent ringing. Disoriented and confused, I struggled to semiconsciousness. For what seemed an eternity, I couldn't identify the source of the sound. The alarm clock! Where was it? My bleary eyes sought the clock. 12:30? Did we set the alarm wrong? Suddenly my mind partially clicked on, and I groped in the dark for the phone. Next to me I felt Dave turn over and half sit up. Who in the world would be phoning at this hour? Oh no, not one of those obscene calls, I prayed. Why did those guys always seem to pick the dead of night? I almost didn't lift the receiver. Then with a rush of anxiety I came fully awake. Our children! Dave's sister and her family! Dave's mother!

"Hello?" I answered.

Silence. Damn-it was an obscene phone call. Just as I started to hang up, I heard what sounded like a whimper. "Mom?"

My stomach lurched. Which daughter was this?

"Mom, it's Sarah." It was our middle daughter, twenty-four years old, and 3000 miles away. Her voice was ghostly, disembodied, and flat.

"Yes, it's me, Honey. What's the matter? Are you all right?" I fought to sound calm.

"I can't go on. I'm cutting my wrists. I called to tell you and Dad goodbye."

Adrenaline panic flooded my body. My heart raced and pounded worse than in an hour of dance aerobics. My throat was so dry I could scarcely speak. I was terrified I'd tip her over the edge. Dave, sensing something was drastically wrong, switched on the bed light. With my hand over the mouthpiece, I gasped, "Sarah says she's cutting her wrists!"

I have little recollection of what happened after that, except that Dave and I took turns on the phone with her for a long time. Finally, Sarah promised to go to sleep. No such luck for us. We held each other like two frightened children. Exhausted with fear and the unknown, we eventually dozed fitfully until daybreak.

The pattern of this first suicidal phone call between midnight and 3:00 A.M. would be repeated many times in the next two years. Mostly the calls came to Dave and me, but Sarah's brother and sisters were also on the receiving end. Dave and I had no prior experience with suicide or hot lines. Until we began to acquire some tools of survival for ourselves, our daily companion would be an almost incapacitating terror. Little did we know that Sarah's phone call would also be the beginning of sixteen long years of family turmoil as Dave and I learned how to live with the disease of addiction in our children.

Up to then, our knowledge about addictive disease was derived from my own personal experience and some limited reading. Until I joined AA, I had never been around another alcoholic as far as I knew, except for a quiet neighbor briefly. If Sarah was an alcoholic, she didn't seem to be a clone of me. I'd certainly not acted "crazy" as her siblings were reporting. After that first suicidal phone call, I was actually more frightened that she might have developed a grave mental illness that would stunt her life, than I was scared about the possibility of alcoholism. My father, a schizophrenic, had died in a mental hospital. I was aware that schizophrenia had a genetic component, and that contributed to my fear.

Nevertheless, I began to read voraciously about the disease of alcoholism to see if Sarah possibly fit the syndrome. The information was essential in broadening Dave's and my understanding of addiction. We began to realize that though the disease has significant predictable commonalities among individuals, it was both futile and dangerous for us as parents to generalize about, or predict, another alcoholic's specific behaviors solely on the basis of one person's experience.

Around that time we heard about intervention, then a relatively new concept. One of my AA friends knew the director of the county alcohol and drug treatment center. He was a trained intervention specialist. Through him Dave and I were introduced to the whole area of professional intervention with alcoholics and addicts. We started to educate ourselves intensively, with the hope that we would be prepared to participate someday in this powerful technique that could save our daughter's life. Betty Ford's first book[1] was published about then, and we took heart from her successful intervention.

After the suicidal phone calls commenced, several friends urged Dave and me to run, not walk, to get additional help for ourselves. We had heard of Al-Anon, and our oldest daughter, Susan, had started attending it in San Francisco when I got sober. However, we were basically ignorant of how Al-Anon worked. One of the women in my alcohol recovery group was married to an active alcoholic and she was a devoted member of Al-Anon. During my first year of sobriety I saw how it was helping to improve her serenity and stability.

Dave wasn't interested in getting involved in such a group on my account, since my recovery was progressing well. Nor did he yet believe Sarah was an alcoholic. I wasn't sure about her, either. Before we left Arlington, we went together to one Al-Anon meeting, but that was it.

As far as I could tell, Dave already appeared to have many of the coping skills recommended by people in Al-Anon: objectivity, fairness, balance, absence of verbal and physical abuse, lack of judgmentalism,

---

1.*The Times of My Life*, Betty Ford, with Chris Chase. Harper & Row. New York. 1978.

and slowness to anger and resentment. Maybe he didn't need a support group. After all, he'd always been an independent, self-reliant man. With these natural strengths, however, he'd developed two survival techniques that would sometimes cause acute distress for himself and others until eventually he overcame them: a tendency to deny what was going on around him, and an unhealthy separation from his own emotions.

I, on the other hand, had yet to learn about the loving detachment that came so naturally to Dave. I was thoroughly enmeshed with my children, to their overall detriment as adults. To my credit, I shed denial about Sarah's possible alcoholism fairly quickly. Also, my own recovery from alcoholism, new though it was, plus the clear evidence of recovery in so many others I saw at AA, gave me a realistic hope that Sarah could recover, too—if, in fact, she was an alcoholic. That was still a question mark.

Shortly before my one-year sober anniversary I flew back to California for a visit to see our children. Late one night our youngest, Rosie, phoned me at the apartment I had sublet for a couple of weeks. She was in tears.

"Mom, Sarah called again, saying she's cutting her wrists. I just can't take it any more. I called the police. Could you go over?"

That horrible adrenaline rush of terror again! I threw on some clothes and ran for the car. Thank God the traffic was light that time of night. Images of blood and a dead or dying daughter choked my breathing. Over and over, like a mantra, I whispered the Serenity Prayer I had learned.

God, grant me the serenity to accept the things I cannot change,
Courage to change the things I can, and
Wisdom to know the difference.

Two police cars were parked outside Sarah's upscale apartment. All her lights were on. The door was locked. I rang the bell. Almost immediately Sarah opened it. Thankfully, she was in one piece, and looked reasonably normal. No bloody wrists! Over her shoulder I saw two police officers watching from the living room.

I gave Sarah a big hug, partly to buy time to think, and was nearly suffocated by the smell of alcohol. In that instant I felt a tremendous surge of relief. My anxiety abruptly vanished. "She *is* an alcoholic!" I thought. "She's not crazy." Alcoholism sounded a lot easier to recover from than some mysterious mental illness. I knew that people could get well from alcoholism.

8

The officers came to the door. I asked if they were aware she'd been drinking. Yes, they said, they had found a nearly empty liquor bottle and a glass on the kitchen drainboard. Soon thereafter they left, apparently satisfied a suicidal crisis had been defused.

As a precaution I decided to stay the rest of the night. Fortunately, Sarah didn't object. It was a long night. Sarah's speech was very slurred and thick, but she was wide awake and talking nonstop. Although she was unsteady on her feet, she was neither belligerent nor "crazy." As her tongue loosened, Sarah rambled on about episodes in her drinking history. As an undergraduate, she "nearly lost it," she said, so disciplined herself not to drink at all for three years, until she graduated.

"No wonder she was so angry all those years," I thought. For a period I had refused to be around her very much because she was so hostile. At the time, I was still drinking myself, and had plenty of hostility of my own to go around. Today, I think how awful it must have been for her to be in a state of constant, albeit unconscious, craving. Who said alcoholics don't have willpower? Without other behavioral and attitudinal changes, however, abstinence could be hell for the alcoholic as well as everyone else.

For the most part, I just listened. At one point, Sarah asked if I thought she was an alcoholic. I told her, yes, and that she probably needed to be in the hospital to detox. Privately, I just wanted her in a safe place until she sobered up, for protection from further suicide attempts. After much stalling, she agreed to call her therapist and let him decide what she should do.

To my utter amazement she managed to pull herself together for that conversation. The slurring vanished. She sounded absolutely normal. If I hadn't seen the transformation with my own eyes, I wouldn't have believed it. Naturally her therapist said that she was all right and to forget going to the hospital. The moment she hung up in triumph all the slurring returned. It was an important lesson in how we can be deceived by alcoholics. If I had been on the other end of the phone, I'd have been fooled, too, despite my own memories of having been able sometimes to act reasonably sober (I think!) while actually very drunk.

I returned to Arlington for the last few months there. Sarah stopped driving a cab and entered a Ph.D. program in Colorado, but the suicidal phone calls kept coming every few weeks and months. Dave and I became increasingly frantic. Our lives were spinning out of control. We felt helpless. I dreaded going to sleep for fear of being wakened by the phone. Then if we were, I couldn't get back to sleep for hours. It was impossible to turn off my imagination. By now we were aware that Sarah was usually drunk when she was suicidal. I had nightmares that one night she would drunkenly cut too deep by accident, pass out from the alcohol, and bleed to death. Yet Dave and I believed and acted as if we could somehow "fix" Sarah ourselves. Wasn't that what parents were for?

My Virginia friends said that when one family member gets sober, the family dynamics shift. How they shifted was unpredictable, but I heard of several spouses who followed a husband or wife into recovery. Dave and I were encouraged from this anecdotal knowledge that other alcoholics in the family were more likely to seek recovery for themselves once the ice was broken. Nevertheless, though my naturally optimistic nature hoped for our daughter's recovery, I didn't dare indulge in expectations. That might tempt an evil fate.

Immediately after my one-year sober anniversary, Dave and I moved back to the Bay Area. We spent a month car-camping across the country. One night in the middle of a forest campground, Dave was abruptly roused by the loud ringing of a telephone. Knowing it must be Sarah, he came wide awake and lunged for the phone, still hearing the ringing clearly. Only there was no phone. In the light of morning, this thoroughly rational engineer remained shaken by the powerful hallucinatory experience. Forced to confront the reality of how he was being affected by our daughter's condition, he was finally willing to find a support group that would "help him save her life." What got to him was not her alcoholism, but the fact that she was attempting suicide. Only then did he realize that all was *not* well. This was really serious! I vowed to start in earnest with a support group, too. It didn't matter whether Sarah was an alcoholic. Something was terribly wrong, and we needed help.

We stopped in Colorado to see Sarah. Though moody, she appeared fairly content for a change. Her graduate work was proceeding well. Dave and I hoped that the new setting would inspire her to stop the suicidal episodes, and at least ease off on the drinking.

Then we swung through Los Angeles to visit our son, Andy. I remember sitting around a picnic table overlooking Pacific Palisades in Santa Monica while we talked about Sarah. I was by now convinced she was an alcoholic, but Andy and Dave both pooh-poohed the idea. None of us fully realized then that men have a particularly hard time

10

admitting that women in general, and especially the women in their own lives, are alcoholics or addicts. The stigma of being a woman alcoholic or addict is still strong. Somehow it's easier for a man to recognize and accept the condition in another male.

Learning to Cope

While Dave and I were settling into our own home again, I began attending alcohol recovery groups and getting acquainted with a new AA community. Once the boxes were unpacked, Dave and I finally went together to Al-Anon. However, since I was one of the two alcoholics in his life, I felt somewhat constrained in his presence, and it seemed as if he could be freer to share honestly without me at his side. We concluded it might be healthier for us to attend separate meetings.

I had resumed part-time teaching at the local community college, and had freedom to choose a daytime meeting. Dave located a newly formed men's group that met at night. These support meetings were lifesavers. In my case, they were an excellent complement and reinforcement to my own alcohol recovery program, right from the start.

Dave was slower to come around. In the beginning he went to Al-Anon not to learn how to control the alcoholic's drinking, as many do, but to save her from death by suicide. It took him a good six months of regular weekly attendance to appreciate the value of Al-Anon (a not uncommon period of time), and to understand that the purpose was to find relief and heal himself, not our daughter. If she found healing, wonderful, but her recovery was ultimately not in our hands.

Each Wednesday for the next eight years, unless I was ill or out of town, I faithfully went to my Al-Anon meeting. Most of the people who came were women with alcoholic or addicted partners or spouses. Their ages ranged from twenty-year-olds to a few in their seventies. A handful of the younger adults were there because of an alcoholic parent, sometimes both parents. The numbers of these adult children of alcoholics (ACAs or ACOAs) increased dramatically in the next few years due to greater research, recognition, and publicity about the prevalence of parental alcoholism and its effects on the children. Separate groups for them sprang up. Some of these adult children discovered they were alcoholics themselves and were in recovery groups for that, too.

11

I valued the stories of ACAs, and began to devour the expanding literature about them in an effort to understand what it must have been like for our own children, since I myself hadn't grown up in an alcoholic home. The flip side was that I steadily saw my own role as an alcoholic mother more clearly, and that often was a source of great sadness.

At first there was only one person in my group who also had an alcoholic child. I listened carefully to how Hannah had learned to ride the roller coaster of daily living with an active alcoholic, and thanked God that at least Sarah wasn't under our roof. In little over a year after I met Hannah, her daughter was becoming so violent and unpredictable that Hannah kept an emergency suitcase packed so she could escape to a friend's when necessary. At last Hannah decided very reluctantly that Dee would either have to move out and break the ties with her mother, or get into recovery. When Hannah asked if I could assist with an informal intervention (see appendix), I was able to repay some of her friendship and support. We were able to convince Dee that she needed to enter a thirty-day hospital recovery program. Thankfully, Dee has remained sober ever since.

Dave found an occasional father of an alcoholic in his men's group. However, the men nearly always came because of an alcoholic wife or girlfriend, not an addicted child.

Unfortunately, our hopes for a change in what we saw as Sarah's suicidal pattern did not come to pass right away. Dave was learning to tolerate the late-night phone calls better than I did, partly because the phone was on my side of the bed! Soon after arriving back home in California, however, I came across a technique that vastly improved my ability to cope with the calls. I named it the instant stress response.[2] All I had to do was take a deep breath, hold it for five seconds, let it out, and repeat once (occasionally a third time). Lo and behold, the adrenaline vanished, and I was instantly calm. It was miraculous.

In our support groups we'd been hearing it was fairly futile to expect a rational conversation with someone who was drunk. Better to talk first thing the next day, before the drinking began again, when the person might be most receptive to reality. Also, though suicide threats must always be taken seriously, it appeared that Sarah didn't really intend to follow through. So, crossing our fingers, we decided

---

2. *The American Way of Life Need Not Be Hazardous to Your Health*, by John W. Farquhar, M.D. W.W. Norton and Company. New York. 1978.

not to talk with her when she called late at night, but instead assure her we'd be in touch the next morning, and end communication immediately. In the morning, of course, we were always careful to check that she was all right.

Dave was able to follow through on this plan without much trouble, but I needed the instant stress response. When the phone rang, I'd take one of those deep breaths, hold it for five seconds, and as I let it out, pick up the receiver. Before Sarah could say anything but her name, I would calmly tell her that we'd talk in the morning, and that I had to go to sleep. Then I'd hang up, take another deep breath, hold it for five seconds, let it out, and fall right back to sleep. A few times she phoned back, disbelieving, but we just repeated the message. It worked! For whatever reason, the crisis calls grew farther and farther apart, and eventually ceased.

This simple technique of the instant stress response has been invaluable in many other stressful situations that simply come along in life—like standing in a slow grocery line when I'm in a hurry, or being cut off on the freeway. I don't know how I ever managed without it.

Sarah's story will be continued later in this account. In the meantime, while she remained a constant concern of greater or lesser immediacy, Dave and I were to encounter unexpected challenges from our other three children. Our stories relating to them are in order of their gaining recovery from addictive disease.

Andy—New Lessons
About Addictive Disease

A teenager during the turbulent sixties, our son, Andy, had spent the year after high school studying drama in England. Upon returning home, he discarded his hippie ways and companions. He became a follower of the Self-Realization Fellowship (SRF) and, at the age of twenty-one, an apprentice monk. At first Dave and I feared SRF might be one of those unsettling cults that seemed to flourish in Los Angeles. We thought we were open-minded, liberal parents, but we were distressed when our son announced his intention of joining SRF. In time, we discovered SRF's honorable history, and came to appreciate its wholesome influence.

Not only did the ashram eschew alcohol and drugs, including tobacco and caffeine, an applicant had to be free of them for two years immediately prior to admission. We didn't suspect how important this was for Andy. Only later did we learn that during high school and for a year or two thereafter, he was a serious marijuana addict who would also indulge in whatever else was around. All this ceased for the two years before he entered the ashram, and the time he was there.

After three years in the ashram, Andy decided to return to lay life. SRF had taken an immature young man and molded him into a thoughtful, disciplined, focused adult. He'd also been taught valuable skills of office management in SRF's huge worldwide printing enterprise. Ever since, I've wondered if most young men and women might profit from a few years of intensive, practical spiritual training like SRF's.

Andy immediately enrolled in college and insisted on supporting himself. He got the first of a series of jobs, and proceeded to live

14

on his own. Then, the summer before his senior year, he started to drive a cab. In the fall he didn't reenroll in school. Instead, he bought his own taxi and continued to drive a cab for several years. He lost contact as a layperson with SRF. His living conditions deteriorated. In fact, when Dave and I visited him on our return from Virginia, we were puzzled and more than a little concerned. He seemed to have dropped all interest in school and reverted to some of his old hippie ways. There was a series of strange girlfriends. He said he didn't need money, though he was currently living in a seedy residential hotel room with the latest lady. But he was in good spirits, so we said goodbye and hoped for the best.

The Christmas I was two years' sober, all the children were home for the holidays. It was during this time that I participated in the intervention with my friend Hannah's daughter. Andy, who was then thirty-one, seemed moderately interested in what happened. The week after he returned to Southern California, Dave and I received a letter from him. He said he was an alcoholic and couldn't deny it any longer. He had started going to a recovery group! We were stunned. As Dave said, "How great to get the solution before we even know the problem!"

Since we were blissfully ignorant of Andy's addictions, we never had to worry about them. We worried about other things, like "Why doesn't he finish college?" and "Is he going to drive a cab the rest of his life?" Whenever he came to visit, of course, he naturally curtailed his alcohol and drug usage. We later learned that within a year of leaving the ashram he resumed addictive patterns of drinking, cigarettes, and marijuana.

Looking back, we were enlightened about the many secondary signs of addiction: an inexplicable economic slide, worsening housing, crazy romantic relationships, a loss of ambition, and the apparent abandonment of formerly strong spiritual interests. With relief and gratitude, we added Andy to our list as we continued learning how to relate to alcoholics in the family. Also, I now had a family "buddy" in recovery from our mutual disease. Dave, however, found the shift more difficult.

Dave was a child of the Great Depression. (So was I, but not in the severely negative way he was.) For him, money was a resource to be husbanded very carefully. (My family didn't have any to be husbanded!) Over the years, money became a potent control issue with Dave as he strove valiantly to keep his family financially above water, never realizing that alcoholism and drug addiction were a significant drain. At the same time, the children and I resented what we considered a needlessly tightwad attitude on his part. When Andy found recovery, Dave and I were well on the road to resolving this issue between ourselves. I became responsible and Dave mellowed. Several years were to elapse, however, before Andy and his father could feel comfortable in relating to each other around the issue of money.

When he was still drinking, for example, Andy called from Los Angeles to say he had a once-in-a-lifetime opportunity to attend a school for future radio announcers, a perfect fit for his talents, but he needed tuition money. We were surprised at the request because he'd been supporting himself by choice. After some agonizing, we sent him around $2,000. We had to borrow the money, so the tuition wasn't an easy thing for us to do. The school went bankrupt before the first class, and Andy told us he couldn't get his money back. Nonetheless, Dave sent Andy monthly statements, insisting on repayment and charging him interest. Payments were erratic. After getting sober, Andy sold his taxi and taxi license at a profit of something like $10,000. Dave coldly demanded immediate payment in full. Andy partially complied. It was not a pleasant situation.

Eventually, when Andy received his bachelor's degree, and had already been sober for several years, Dave felt much differently about money. Also, we knew that Andy had become a responsible manager of money. We forgave the remaining debt on the earlier tuition loan as part of a graduation gift.

Many years later, Andy confessed that he did get his tuition money back, and said how sorry he was about the whole episode. He had felt guilty about it all that time, and offered to repay the debt we'd forgiven as a graduation gift long before. Surprised, we were also gratified that he was continuing to clean up any remaining wreckage of his past by making "amends wherever possible," as the 12-step programs advise. We thanked him, but felt there was no need to repay us. He'd discharged his responsibility by being honest and making an honest offer. Since then, Andy and his father have been able to discuss financial issues openly and comfortably, without any hidden agendas.

From our distance in northern California, Andy's recovery seemed steady. Active in AA during early sobriety, he then lost contact with it for many years, but stayed sober, nevertheless. Initially, I was concerned that he might relapse, and was often tempted to offer unsolicited advice. Dave and I had plenty of practice in "zipping our lips" as I, in particular, continued to learn gradually how to "let go" and not try to control a person or outcome. Last year, Andy suddenly returned wholeheartedly to AA. One never knows!

After several years of sobriety, Andy married Karen, a lovely nonalcoholic, who had participated in Al-Anon for several years during her first marriage, to another alcoholic. Andy was finally motivated to sell his cab and complete both his undergraduate and master's degrees. He and Karen have a little girl. Ann is a blessed child. Not only will she probably never have to endure an actively alcoholic parent, she also benefits from Andy's growth in recovery. No one knows if Ann carries the gene (or genes) of alcoholism, but at least she can never blame her formative environment. As grandparents, Dave and I are very thankful that the destructive pattern of addiction may be permanently broken for our only grandchild. Andy and Karen own their own home, and Andy has taught high school English and drama in a large urban school system for many years. He's been clean and sober since January 1980.

A few years ago Dave hung up the phone after chatting with Andy and Karen, and scared me with an odd, gasping sound. I turned from the couch to look at him, and realized he was crying. That alarmed me even more, because in forty-some years of marriage, I'd never seen my husband cry. He sat down beside me, and I put my arms around him, thinking something awful must have happened between him and Andy. Instead, it turned out his sobs were of joy. Andy had just told him how much he loved him, and how he wanted his dad to know he always had a place in Andy's home. It was a true miracle of healing.

Andy's Perspective

An overriding concern while I was a practicing alcoholic, and later on as a recovering one, has been my fear of letting others find out who I am. I've been so afraid that if others really knew me, they wouldn't like me at all, so I've found it necessary to construct a "likeable" persona: Andy who's OK, in control of his life, and always competent. Inside, I felt I had no control over my life and was scared to death that others would somehow "see through" my self-constructed armor of self-confidence.

One of my biggest fears was that my parents would find out that I could not handle life at all and that they would discover that alcohol had become the only way I knew to cope with life. To be exposed to my parents as an adult who could not function in the adult world was deeply frightening to me. After all, my parents were the very people who had always loved me unconditionally (a kind of love I never really understood until I became a father myself). If they stopped loving me, then all was lost. I went to great lengths, therefore, to hide my alcoholism from my parents.

That wasn't a difficult task while my mother was still a practicing alcoholic. Her own alcoholic behavior, as well as that of my sisters, provided a convenient diversion from my own disease. However, when my mother got sober and began practicing an active program of recovery, my fear of being "found out" deepened. I tried to put on the mask of self-confidence. I remember telling my parents, "I've never been happier," during one of their visits to me while I was essentially jobless, about to turn thirty, living in a $25 a week room in Hollywood, and cohabiting with a girlfriend who was a jobless high school dropout. My mother writes that I was "in good spirits." In reality, I felt my life crumbling beneath my feet.

Two things finally drove me to recovery. One was my mother's own sobriety and the positive changes brought about in her life as a result of recovery from alcoholism. I felt that if she could be helped, perhaps there was hope for me, too. The other was that my life took a decided turn for the worse. Events began happening that I felt could not possibly go unnoticed by my parents. One confused girlfriend traveled 500 miles, unannounced, to visit my parents. Another girl phoned them to say how screwed up I was. I felt that my cover was blown. That was really when I began to hit bottom—when I felt that my disease was so uncontrollable I could no longer successfully conceal it from my parents. They, however, never gave any indication that they were judging or turning against me. I still felt their love, and this was very important to me. If they thought my life was a mess, they never said so. They didn't have to. I already knew.

I'll never forget one particular visit I made to my parents about this time. There was a quiet-spoken man about my age visiting for the afternoon. My mother introduced him as a friend who was a member of AA. This young man proceeded to tell me about himself and the disease of alcoholism. He never gave any hint that he knew I could be an alcoholic, but I absorbed his every word. Two weeks later I joined AA myself and got sober.

My parents note that my recovery "seemed steady." Initially, I threw myself wholeheartedly into the process of recovery. I loved sobriety. Then, although I continued not to drink, I began to drift away from AA meetings. My recovery felt anything but steady. I stayed sober in spite of myself because I didn't want to look like a failure by drinking again. The disgrace would have been more than I could bear. By this time, not only was my mother sober, but two of my sisters also. I got married and had a daughter. The idea of throwing away my new family terrified me. Which isn't to say I wasn't tempted to drink. I sometimes was. Yet my own stubbornness and self-centeredness kept me from turning for help to the very program that saved me in the first place.

I also stayed sober by becoming a workaholic. Then, several things happened all at once. My father-in-law, who had lived next door, died after a long illness. Karen, Ann, and I moved to a new community and bought our first house. I switched job sites, and my wife began to work full time. My life was suddenly totally unmanageable.

So after fifteen years of sobriety, I went back to the beginning and started attending AA regularly. I asked for help, and got it. I began—finally—to drop the mask of self-control I'd worn for so long. I admitted I was powerless.

Today I am so grateful to my parents and my sisters. My mother and sisters got sober and, for a long time, they were my only connection to a recovery program. I believe they kept me sober without even knowing they were.

Rosie—the Challenge of Intervention

Over the next two years Dave and I noticed that our youngest daughter, Rosie, seemed to be going nowhere with her life. We wondered if we were expecting too much of our children. Rosie had always seemed bright, but in high school she'd rebelled scholastically. The only way she was able to graduate was by attending "continuation school" for her senior year. We had no idea that a large part of the problem was due to drug use and heavy drinking. There was one occasion, however, that could have raised a red flag for us about the possibility of addiction in Rosie if we hadn't been so ignorant and in such parental denial.

Needing a break, Dave and I went camping by ourselves for a weekend. Rosie was sixteen, and the only child still living at home. A family friend, whom Dave and I called an "honorary son," was visiting. Jack was then about twenty, and a hippie free spirit in some ways. Dave and I felt comfortable about leaving Rosie and Jack to hold the fort for a couple of days. We told them to expect us back in the late afternoon on Sunday.

Unfortunately, the campground gave me a bad case of sneezing allergies, so we packed up a few hours early on Sunday and headed home. When we walked into the house before noon, we went into shock. The house was a mess. So was the yard. Litter, overflowing ashtrays, and beer cans were all over the place. There were stains on the carpet. The house reeked of stale smoke and booze. Every bed in the five-bedroom house had been used, including ours. One stray teenager was still passed out on a bed. Dave was so mad, he grabbed him awake, and threw him out the front door before the kid knew what was happening. It's the only time I've ever seen Dave lose his temper like that.

Rosie and Jack, who we later realized were severely hungover, were trying to clean up before we got home. In the end, they filled several thirty-gallon trash barrels with empty beer cans, wine bottles, hard-liquor bottles, plastic cups, half-empty bags of chips, and all the other detritus of a big, wild party. Neighbors on the cul-de-sac told us there'd been a lot of noise into the wee hours, but apparently thought we were at home. At one point they saw a couple making out on top of a van parked in front of our driveway. Why the neighbors never complained, or called the police, was a mystery. Recently Rosie told us that some of the "guests" climbed onto the roof and dived into the swimming pool below. Thank God it was the deep end and also that they didn't hit the five-foot-wide concrete deck.

We were furious with Rosie and Jack. I felt that our home had been defiled. Rosie said the party started out with a small group that got out of hand—as unsupervised teenage bashes have a way of doing. She didn't know what to do when friends of friends of friends, followed by total strangers, kept arriving. Jack, who certainly should have known better, was a washout as chaperon. Both Rosie and Jack joined the growing crowd instead of throwing them out or calling someone for help.

For more than a year, Dave had been quietly agitating to sell our big house and find a smaller one with less maintenance and yard work since the three older children were gone. I had resisted, but now I was so upset I impulsively agreed. I couldn't wait to get out of the house.

Unsupervised teenage parties today can have far more drastic consequences than did Rosie's. In retrospect, we're very grateful that back then there were no guns or gangs in suburban neighborhoods. Nor HIV and AIDS. Nor was anything burglarized or vandalized, as often happens now.

Could Dave and I have done something to arrest Rosie's addiction at that stage of her life? Maybe, if I'd been sober and Dave less affected by the family disease. We didn't know then what we know today about addictive disease. It simply never occurred to Dave and me at the time to look at Rosie's drinking as a contributing factor. We didn't suspect that she already had a well-established pattern of drinking and using drugs. All we saw and overreacted to was this single example of unacceptable behavior. Ten years were to pass before the blinders lifted from our eyes regarding Rosie. She would go through much worse, more dangerous, situations than a free-for-all teenage party.

Following high school, Rosie halfheartedly tried community college and managed to accumulate a few credits. Then she dropped out and went to work as a security guard, where she met her first husband. After I got sober I realized Jake was very likely an alcoholic. Then at one point her mother-in-law called us to express her concern about Rosie's drinking. This was news to Dave and me, but somehow I wasn't surprised. Mindful of the lessons in Al-Anon and AA, we didn't intervene—yet. We just watched from a distance, and waited.

That summer Rosie temporarily moved in with us, and divorced her husband of four years. There were no children. She took an entry level job at a local fast-food shop and began a series of moves to stay ahead of successive apartment landlords. Eventually she ended up living with a man in a trashy house in a nearby ghetto that was notorious for guns, violence, and drugs.

Her housemate was of course her drug supplier as well as lover. We didn't know that she was freebasing cocaine (this was in the days before crack) and drinking alcoholically. Since the only two items of furniture in the house were a mattress on the floor and a completely stocked bar in the living room, you'd think we could have figured it out. We might have continued to let matters take their own course, even though it was increasingly painful to be around a visibly disintegrating daughter who was turning brittle and distant, if we hadn't been brought up short by an unexpected development.

While Rosie was still married, Dave had cosigned a loan with her and Jake for a few thousand dollars. Rosie assured her father periodically that she was taking care of the payments even though she and Jake were now divorced. Then one day the finance company phoned Dave as the cosigner to demand immediate payment on a delinquent debt of over a year. Rosie hadn't been making any payments at all during that time. By now Dave and I had a saner attitude about money, so the issue for us wasn't financial. What threw us was the deceit in a daughter whom we'd had no reason to distrust. Moreover, such action seemed out of character for her. How naive we were!

Thank God, for what we had learned thus far in our recovery groups. We knew we mustn't gallop to her rescue. Though we had scarcely any direct personal evidence of her drinking, we were wiser about the secondary signs of alcoholism. I remembered the question my Virginia friends had asked about Sarah four years before, "Does she have a drinking problem?" Secretly I phoned a couple of Rosie's friends for information. They confirmed that she was a very active alcoholic indeed.

Dave and I decided that intervention might halt her increasingly precipitous slide. Her employers at the fast-food place were dismayed to hear of her condition. However, they said there was insurance coverage for hospital treatment since Rosie was now an assistant manager, and they promised not to say anything to her about our intervention intentions.

With a gulp and a prayer, Dave and I talked with a professional intervention counselor. The purpose of an intervention is to breach a person's powerful denial system through a concerted addressing of the problem in a single session by a group composed of all the family and/or friends closest to the intervenee. It is nearly impossible to get past an alcoholic's defense system one-on-one. Alcoholics can rationalize an individual's objections out of existence.

Besides intervening as a united group, the second essential element in a successful intervention is surprise. Secrecy must be maintained by the participants until the intervenee is actually in the room for the event. The shock of unexpected confrontation with everyone who knows some piece of one's drinking history, and hearing the whole story come together, is usually sufficient to overcome massive denial in the alcoholic. The third element is careful, detailed planning with a trained professional intervention counselor.

We went by the book.[1] For six weeks before and after Christmas the family prepared in secret for the intervention. Even though no one had much that was concrete to report, each of us wrote what we had observed or experienced as a result of Rosie's drinking, and stated how we felt about each episode. Our counselor required us to express it all with love and no judgmentalism. She carefully edited our statements and coached us separately and together. We were told that there could be no ad-libbing. We were to read only what we had written. My written report took the most editing of anyone's because I was so "preachy." After several tries, the intervention counselor finally pronounced my words acceptable.

We reserved a bed at a hospital treatment center thirty miles away, intending to put distance between Rosie and her drug-dealer boyfriend. The idea was to hold the intervention, then if she agreed, to take her there immediately while her denial system was still down. We were advised that a well-organized professional intervention had

---

1.Our classic guide was *I'll Quit Tomorrow,* Revised Edition. Vernon E. Johnson. Harper & Row. New York. 1980. The updated version is *Training Families to Do a Successful Intervention: A Professional's Guide.* Johnson Institute. Minneapolis, MN. 1996.

a success rate of at least 80 percent. However, we were each asked to decide what the consequences would be in our separate relationships with Rosie in case the intervention failed.

We don't remember what our other children concluded for themselves, but Dave and I resolved that if Rosie refused help, we nevertheless could not banish her from our lives. But in order to mitigate the pain in watching her fall apart, we would have to limit our contact and specify the limits clearly to her. Also, we wouldn't enable her with any financial support.

Andy came up from Southern California, and Susan down from the City. Sarah couldn't make the trip from Colorado, unfortunately, but she'd written her statement. Dave was delegated to get Rosie to the appointed place and time without giving away the reason until she was in the room with us and the counselor. For all we knew, she'd refuse to go with her dad, or run when she saw the rest of us. At the last minute, Susan got cold feet and nearly backed out. In fact, when I went to meet her train, I didn't know whether she'd be on it, but she was.

Rosie's supervisor at the fast-food place had been a party to planning the intervention, but she decided some days before that she would not participate in the event itself. However, she was able to cooperate in the "kidnapping." She knew when Rosie's dad was coming to pick her up and made sure that Rosie would be available.

It was a regular day at work for Dave, but he found it increasingly difficult to keep his mind on his work as it got closer to the time when he had to leave work, get in the car, and drive a few miles to Rosie's place of work. Those moments, until Rosie was in the car, were the most anxious for Dave, and the time when he thought the intervention was at its greatest risk. If he could get her into the car and begin the drive to the family meeting, then the plan would unfold. But if, for some reason, Rosie refused to go with her dad, the intervention would be a failure before it started.

Dave had rehearsed his part in his mind over and over. He knew just what he was going to do and say. In a way, it was a relief to play out the part. He did his lines as he had practiced them.

"Rosie, we have a family emergency and I want you to come with me to join the rest of the family for a meeting." That was all he had to say.

Rosie complied. On the way, Dave remained silent (not unusual for him) in answer to all of Rosie's questions. "What is the emergency?" "Where are we going?" "Who's going to be there?"

Dave was relieved that the most critical part for him had come off all right. Although he was tempted to respond to Rosie's questions, he realized that the only way he'd be sure to get to the meeting and keep the surprise was if he said nothing. If he started answering questions, who knows where they might lead?

When they turned into the parking lot, one of Rosie's questions, "Where?" was answered. Now came another risky time, going from the car to the meeting room. Rosie could still bolt. Dave just said, "We're meeting in a room down this way."

Like the ride in the car, the walk was silent. When he opened the door and they walked in the room, Dave was finally able to let go a little, because the part that depended on him alone had succeeded. Now it was a group activity and everyone knew his or her part—except Rosie.

In debriefing later, we interveners concluded Dave had the trickiest and most fearful task of all, yet he managed to carry it off without once disclosing to Rosie the reason for "kidnapping" her from her job, or telling her where they were going. I don't think I could even have driven the car!

We had arranged to meet in the intervention counselor's office, which just happened to be located at the end of a hospital psych ward, but with no other connection to psychiatry. As the hour approached, the tension was excruciating. I couldn't even make small talk to distract myself. Instead I went into a kind of numb state. I knew we were fighting for Rosie's life the best we knew how, but the three of us—Susan, Andy, and myself—waiting there with the counselor, later reported painfully churning stomachs and clammy hands. Finally, Dave walked in with Rosie, and we all breathed a deep sigh of relief. That hurdle was over.

The counselor told Rosie what was happening. She was asked to listen to each statement without any comment. When all the statements were finished, she could have her say. Our counselor had predetermined the order in which we were to read. I was last. I watched Rosie's expression as she heard her brother, her sister, and her father. Her face got harder and stonier. Inside I despaired that the intervention was lost. As I started to read, my voice shook and I began to cry, but I plowed on to the end. When I looked up, Rosie was in tears.

"Yes, I know I need help," she said. She put up a token resistance to hospitalization, but we were home free.

To our dismay, Rosie's drug dealer promptly moved up to the City to be close to her. When she was discharged from the hospital after completing her month-long treatment program, they lived together once more, this time in the City. For three months, Rosie didn't go to aftercare at the hospital or attend AA. By some miracle, she stayed clean and sober. The whole family marveled at her continuing abstinence, but feared it couldn't last. Thanks to our programs, Dave and I were able to honestly pray for her continuing health, let go, and turn her over to the care of her Higher Power. I had no energy to do more.

Then Rosie's boyfriend announced he'd like to add another woman to their living arrangement. He would "love" both equally. At that Rosie had the sense to say, no thanks, and leave. She returned to live with us—finally, to our relief, becoming involved in AA, which has sustained and enriched her ever since. She pursued a two-year community college program in X-ray technology, then specialized in mammography. She's also a certified breastcare educator.

I, too, returned to school at the age of sixty, this time to a seminary to prepare for the ministry with the objective of becoming a hospital chaplain. Rosie and I were very busy with our studies, but we all pitched in and lived together in amazing harmony. She discovered she had brains, including an aptitude for math, and bounced through her subjects with enthusiasm. The two years she lived at home are a precious memory.

Dave had some fears beforehand because he and Rosie were at constant loggerheads when she was in high school. However, he had learned in Al-Anon how to relate to her as one adult to another, and was very successful in applying himself. He had realized several years before, through the men in his Al-Anon group, that he'd spent most of our marriage unable to recognize his own emotions, and had instead lived them primarily through me, but also through our children. Whatever any one of us felt, he did, too. It could be exasperating. When Rosie came back to live with us, Dave was well on the way to independent awareness of himself. This was as refreshing for her as for him.

While she was living with us, Rosie met her wonderful second husband, Trent, in AA. From the day of her intervention, despite many ups and downs, including the onset of kidney cancer in Trent (and at present spontaneous regression!), Rosie has remained clean and sober since January 1982, and a delight to all who know her.

Dave and I are enormously thankful that we had educated ourselves about intervention, though we never dreamed of using it with anyone but Sarah. It's the scariest thing I've ever done. Rosie herself, in telling her story, becomes very emotional when she describes the intervention from her then frightened yet ultimately deeply grateful perspective. She recounts how she was actually praying that someone would notice the difficulty she was in and help her. I think Dave and I heard her prayer without realizing it.

Rosie's Experience

I never knew that my mother was an alcoholic. She began drinking right after I was born, so for me, it was as natural as the sunrise every morning. It didn't dawn on me that other mothers didn't drink like she did.

Our household was never violent or messy or embarrassing. A nutritious dinner was on the table every night. My parents were prosperous and happy and kind. That this family spawned five alcoholics and one raging codependent (my father) never struck me as odd while I was living in it. I just had a mother who passed out in front of the TV every night.

As the baby of the family, I learned from my older sisters and brother that drinking and using drugs as a teenager was an acceptable thing to do. I had an abnormal capacity to hold my liquor. Drinking was the normal way of things to me.

By the time I was twenty-one I was a daily drinker. I had graduated from beer and wine to bourbon, and had learned to tolerate wrenching hangovers. I had, unfortunately, graduated from little else. I barely squeaked out of high school. College was out of the question. I definitely had not graduated from adolescence into adulthood. Responsibility was a concept that went right over my head. I was working in a dead-end job headed for nowhere.

My circumstances, though, didn't alarm me. It was the way I felt that concerned me. I lacked self-confidence and self-esteem. I was awkward and unsure of myself. I yearned for whatever it was that other young twenty-somethings had—whatever it was that made them fall in love and have children, or strive for promotion or higher degrees in college, to forge ahead in their lives with a calm and confidence that I so sorely lacked.

When I was twenty-two, my mother stopped drinking and said she was an alcoholic. Outwardly I was supportive, but inside I was resentful. She had taught me, by example, to drink, and here she was saying, "Oops! Sorry, I was wrong ...."

Over the next four years I continued to drink and my circumstances continued to decline. I sat back helplessly as every single member of my family sought recovery, even my sister Sarah for a brief period. All I could do was steal more money from the cash register at work and buy another bottle of bourbon on the way home.

By the time I was twenty-six, I was dead inside—spiritually and emotionally dead. I felt nothing but the daily hangover. I was living with a drug dealer and hanging out with murderers, thieves, and other dealers.

A month before I got sober, I attended midnight services on Christmas Eve. I remember singing hymns and looking around me at all those parishioners, their faces lit up by the spark of faith. Tears came to my eyes as I sang because I had no idea what they were feeling. I wanted desperately to feel what they did, to have a spiritual life that seemed unattainable to me. I reached my bottom then, singing in church, knowing I might never know the joy I saw in everyone else that night. My family had no idea how I really felt. They only saw my miserable circumstances. It's ironic that my family taught me to drink and use, and it was my family that finally intervened.

A professional intervention is very scary for the alcoholic. At least it was for me. At 3:00 in the afternoon my father came to the fast-food place where I worked and said, "Let's go." He took my hand and led me out the door. I was raised to do as he said, so I went. In the car he wouldn't tell me where we were going. All he said was, "Don't worry. Everybody's all right." As he drove along, I got more and more anxious. What was happening?

Finally we arrived at a hospital. Why here? My father still wouldn't say anything. We began walking down a corridor marked with yellow lines. A sign said to follow these lines to the psych ward. We kept following the lines right to the doors and into that unit. My heart sank like a stone. Now I knew—I was crazy, and my father was committing me!

Numbly I followed him through the unit to an office at the very end, where I found my mother, brother, older sister, and a counselor. My other sister was in Colorado. My family didn't look happy, but they acted kindly. Each one in turn read me a letter, giving specific instances in which my drinking and lying were a problem. I remember the word "alcoholic" being bandied about, but through my tears, all I could admit to was a "drinking problem." My family lovingly told me that they had taken care of everything with my employers and my insurance; there was a bed waiting for me in a thirty-day treatment program if I chose to go. Embarrassed and puzzled by the relief I felt, I went—after a quick stop at home to collect some clothes and hurriedly tell my boyfriend goodbye.

It was only later that I realized I had been waiting for somebody to do something. Because everyone else in the family was familiar with alcohol recovery and family support programs, I had often seen literature lying about. The only thing that had sunk in through my alcohol haze was the concept of powerlessness. I understood that I was powerless over alcohol so I waited for someone to rescue me. I didn't understand I could seek help on my own.

My family seemed to sense that and used the powerful tool of intervention to break through to me. I felt like a deer caught in the headlights until they slammed on the brakes and let me live again. I cry writing about it even now. By the grace of God I am still clean and sober, fourteen years later.

I've been sober now for as long as I drank. I finally feel the self-confidence and calm self-assurance I was so jealous of in my peers. At forty, I'm like a twenty-six-year-old, except now I have the wisdom of experience to temper the bravado. I fell in love and am married to the most wonderful man on earth. Even his diagnosis of terminal cancer hasn't made me pick up a bottle of bourbon. Life is too precious.

I wouldn't change a day of my life before I got sober. Every drink, every lower companion, and every financial problem got me to where I am today, and every day has given me the gift of sobriety—a gift from the family that taught me to drink.

Susan—Stuns and Baffles Us

For the next few months, following the intervention, we enjoyed a period of relative calm. Our oldest child, Andy, and youngest, Rosie, had found recovery and were solidly on the road to health. My fifth sober anniversary was at hand. Even Sarah had decided to try AA and was again temporarily sober.

Susan, our elder daughter, had been in Al-Anon for nearly five years. I was enormously grateful that at least one of our children had escaped the disease of alcoholism. She and Dave faithfully attended their respective recovery groups, as did I. In retrospect, it was but a lull before the storm. Looking back, should we have seen it coming?

Susan, the next oldest child to Andy, had had some very trying years growing up. A gifted child, she'd been advanced two grades in elementary school, eventually graduating from high school with honors when only fifteen. Then she was off to college, more than able to handle the intellectual side, but—as we were belatedly to recognize—socially immature and out of synch with her peers. We were, however, unaware that from high school on Susan had experimented with drugs as her siblings had, though never to their extremes. Dave and I believed there were simply social maturation issues to be concerned about with her.

Dave and I had been personally blessed most of our lives with the rewards of achievement, certainly scholastically. Like many such parents, we set high standards and had high expectations for our children. I basked in their academic successes, feeling that the glory reflected on me, too. When Susan, the family's designated "brain," suddenly became a low and even nonachiever at one of the country's finest universities, I took it as a personal affront. I became very angry at what I perceived as betrayal.

Eventually, following a couple of false starts, Susan managed to get her bachelor's degree (in art history), yet seemed unable to advance from there. She moved back home with us, but was very depressed and lethargic. She became noticeably overweight. (Since adolescence Susan had struggled with an increasing overweight that is almost certainly genetic in my family, not Dave's.)

Coincidentally, I was also approaching the last two or three years of my drinking, and had developed a "trigger tongue" and temper to match. I had also become very fat, yet ignored my own condition as I persisted in hounding Susan about her weight. For his part, Dave retreated ever more into silence and isolation in order to escape from the escalating emotional chaos in the family. Needless to say, neither Dave nor I had a clue what to do about Susan. We couldn't even recognize what was the matter with us, much less take care of anyone else.

After months of waiting to see if Susan would snap out of her lethargy, we finally told her in harsh terms that she would have to find a place of her own and either get schooling in an employable skill or simply find a job. She was twenty-one years old and we didn't intend to support her. She moved to the City and enrolled in commercial art, but remained somewhat depressed and listless. Dave and I were so concerned about her that we seriously debated not moving to Virginia, feeling she needed us as an anchor. Some anchor! Fortunately for all concerned, as it turned out, we went ahead with the move since we couldn't see how staying in the Bay Area would help.

During the two years we were gone, Susan more or less drifted. She took courses in commercial art, then dropped out and began working at temporary secretarial jobs, primarily in the City's financial district. When I got sober in Virginia, however, she began attending Al-Anon regularly.

After Dave and I returned to the Bay Area, Susan resumed her emotional and social dependence on us. She continued temporary clerical work, and was able to earn a steady, if modest, income. Although she was making new friends through Al-Anon, her social life seemed fairly lonely to us, except for Saturday evenings she spent with a girlfriend at a bar/nightclub that specialized in Brazilian music and dancing.

Then, eight months after Rosie's intervention, Susan called.

"Are you sitting down, Mom?"

"Oh, oh," I thought, "what now?"

"I'm an alcoholic and I've started going to AA. It's the best thing I've ever done!"

Dave and I were absolutely stunned. We would have bet our bottom dollar that Susan was not an alcoholic. Quiet, reserved, and brainy, she strongly resembled her moderate, careful father. She just didn't fit my picture of even the solitary, private woman drinker. Dave and I were shocked to realize that all four of our children were now identified with addictive disease. The two youngest we had recognized (Sarah and Rosie), the two oldest we hadn't (Andy and Susan).

Susan went on to say that she was tired of trying to control her drinking. "I know I have a high bottom compared with most people in recovery, but I've seen where this road has taken the rest of my family and I don't want to go any further down it."

What a relief, Dave and I thought, once more to have the solution to alcoholism before we even knew there was a problem. One more reason now, we ruefully reflected, to keep going to Al-Anon. But after all the intervention stress surrounding Rosie, Susan sounded like a piece of cake. Moreover, Andy's and Rosie's recoveries had generally been pleasant and upbeat for us. We looked forward to more of the same with Susan. Dave and I congratulated ourselves that we were experienced in relating to both active and recovering alcoholic adult children.

Hindsight is a great teacher. It was clear that five years in Al-Anon had compelled Susan, like others we've known, to confront her own increasing drinking. In trying to reconstruct clues we'd missed about her alcoholism, I recalled a trip to her studio apartment one time to pick up some clothes and personal items for her when she was hospitalized briefly. I was surprised to notice six or eight wine glasses and tumblers scattered around, some with a few dregs of wine or whiskey. I knew there had been no party. But her emergency hospitalization took precedence in my mind, and I pushed this odd piece of information to the back burner.

About the same time she joined AA, Susan also discovered Overeaters Anonymous, a 12-step recovery program for people who share various eating disorders. In her customary thorough way, she applied their suggestions wholeheartedly. The consequence has been more than a decade of a hopefully permanent release from years of excessive weight.

Shortly after Susan stopped drinking, we were delighted to see her become reenergized. She enrolled in an MBA program (Master in business administration) at a major local university. She was busy, so we didn't see much of her. We became gradually aware, however, of an atypical prickliness in her. Our expectations of an easy recovery for Susan were soon demolished. She stayed sober, but her personality seemed to change for the worse. Formerly sweet-natured and the most accommodating of our children, she was more and more hostile and difficult to be around. By the time she graduated, we weren't even sure she'd invite us to the ceremony.

Much of the problem turned out to be long-suppressed anger and resentment at having grown up in an alcoholic household. Once she stopped drinking, she could no longer mask these memories and feelings. Because she herself wanted to find relief, Susan became intensively involved in adult children of alcoholics (ACA) groups, and at one point sought individual professional counseling. Our other children haven't seemed as adversely affected by my years of drinking. Perhaps Susan was at an especially vulnerable adolescent age when my alcoholism began to peak.

After receiving her MBA, Susan started working close to where we lived. Our relationship was a disaster. If we happened to be at the same AA meeting, she pointedly turned her back or moved a distance away, and spoke with others. She couldn't tolerate being around any of us in the family, except for Dave, but I felt I was a special target of dislike that verged on hate. Dave would meet Susan for breakfast at a restaurant every week or two, in order to maintain minimal contact. Even with him, she'd often erupt and leave in the middle of the meal. His patience and understanding seemed phenomenal to me.

If it hadn't been for my ACA friends in Al-Anon and AA, I don't know how I would have survived. Part of me understood and ached for Susan and for my role in the delayed effect on her. At the same time, I wanted to scream, "But you're a recovering alcoholic yourself! Why can't you understand? And I'm not like that anymore!"

One day, in my Al-Anon meeting, I was so angry at her behavior, I announced to the group that I was going to force her to talk to me and have it out. I still believed that as a mother I was entitled to respect and some degree of control over what seemed to me a willful, uncivil daughter who should know better (but who was also in her late twenties, living on her own, and free to choose her own attitudes and relationships).

Thank goodness for the ACAs. They promptly squashed my idea for confrontation, saying it would only make matters worse. They knew from their own experience. Instead, they reassured me that Susan was going through a normal phase in the ACA healing process, upsetting as it was for us, and someday she'd come out the other side. I yearned to believe them, but also struggled to resign myself to possibly a lifetime of hate and rejection. In fact, several of our friends in AA did have one or more adult children who had chosen to disengage with uncompromising anger from them and often siblings as well. Permanent estrangement was a dreadful prospect.

We knew this phase of recovery must be very painful for Susan, too, but at the time it was hard to feel sympathy. Today I admire the guts it took for her to stay the course. I'm reminded of biblical psalmists who, like her, demand that God, or someone, pay attention. But it was excruciatingly difficult for me to stay backed off and let others be the agents of healing—especially since in my case the motive and approach would more accurately have been "righteous correction," not healing.

By the Christmas of 1984, Susan had been sober over two years. As I was wrapping presents, suddenly I burst into tears as I realized that anything I might give her would likely be received with silent, ill-concealed hostility, perhaps not even accepted or opened. It was an utterly helpless, hopeless feeling. Dave tried to comfort me but I was inconsolable at the loss of a child. It felt like a living death. This was the absolute bottom for me.

The next day as I was writing my fears and grief in a journal, there suddenly came into overwhelming memory the image of Susan as the wonderful, cherished infant she'd been. All my resentment towards her behavior of the past two years was swept away in tears of unconditional love. Without regret I relinquished the last vestiges of illusion that I had the power or desire to control my children, or any other adult person for that matter. With total confidence and a full heart, I turned Susan over to the care of her Higher Power. Susan appeared to remain the same. Nothing changed except me. I continued to feel recurrent sadness, but I was at peace.

Dave's spiritual life was also being affected by Susan. About this time, one of his support groups asked him to lead a discussion on his understanding of God or a Higher Power. Not having given the subject much more than casual thought, he was at first apprehensive about what he could say. The more he considered what he believed, however, the more he realized how deep was his faith in some kind of Power. His thought process was typically rational. As he describes it, he recalled how as a boy he would go swimming in the southern California ocean with his father. They would dive beneath the breakers and swim out to the deeper water, there to be rocked in "the cradle of the deep," supported by the great power of a benign sea.

Then Dave reflected how limited was his personal power on a daily basis. All the processes of his body that kept him alive went on without his supervision or conscious awareness. His job was to contribute to the healthy maintenance of himself in whatever ways necessary. He also truly grasped that he had even less power over other human beings or events. From that moment he was able to surrender his life and will to cooperate with a Power greater than himself.

Suddenly, out of the blue, with no forewarning, Susan called one summer day and asked if she could stay with us for a few weeks until she moved to Los Angeles to pursue some additional schooling. Dave and I were flabbergasted but delighted. It was as if she'd abruptly walked out of a dark forest into the sunshine and has been there ever since. Until Susan read this account, Dave and I had no inkling of what, if anything, precipitated her change of heart. We never asked. Strangely enough, it truly didn't seem to matter. Her remarks following this section reflect another miracle of healing in our family's odyssey.

That fall Susan moved permanently to southern California. After several adventures, she found her niche at last in a well-deserved national management position with an international corporation. She, too, met a wonderful husband, Alex, in AA. One of my life's greatest joys was being asked to conduct their wedding not long after I was ordained. I wish we lived closer. I cherish the adult friendship, love, and regard Susan and I have for one another, and my heart is filled with thanksgiving for the healing of what once seemed an impossible rupture. Luckily, Susan never relapsed during her early painful years of recovery from both alcoholism and being an ACA. She has been sober from the start, August 1982.

Susan's Account

When I stopped drinking, I had some resentments toward people that seemed to demand hours of my thinking time and left me little peace of mind. I sought the advice of a woman who had stopped drinking a long time ago, and she told me to pray for all of them and to pursue a spiritual life. I didn't like this advice, but I wanted to stay sober, so I tried to follow it as well as I could. I prayed every day that the best would happen for everyone I had a resentment toward, even though I didn't really feel like it.

Somehow I felt that I'd been cheated by life. My mother had been a noticeably practicing alcoholic from the time I was eight years old, and I was angry about that. I was the typical ACA, or adult child of an alcoholic, angry about the whole alcoholic family scene, even though I knew I loved my parents a lot. I was angry that I didn't have a decent role model when I was a teenager, that I got blamed for the trouble my younger sisters got into, and that I had to be responsible for so many things because I was the eldest girl.

So I got into an ACA-oriented therapy group, where we all talked about living with alcoholics and how treacherous an experience it was. Several group members no longer maintained contact with family members who were still drinking. I felt particularly vulnerable and emotional every time I was with my own family, even though my mother was in recovery. It was difficult to integrate fourteen years' experience of living with her as an alcoholic with the new and wonderful woman she had become in sobriety. I was tremendously grateful for her sobriety, but it didn't automatically erase the past for me.

I resolved to stay away from the family for awhile, until I'd gotten through the roughest part of therapy. I wanted time to focus on some of the past issues I had with my parents. I knew it was only temporary and that eventually things would work out. I decided to skip one Thanksgiving and maybe one Christmas. I didn't really think I'd be missed that much. I didn't realize until much later that it actually hurt my mother quite a bit.

The prayers finally worked. I woke up one day when I was two years sober, and the worst of my resentments toward my parents were gone. I have no explanation, they were just gone. Then I moved to the place where my parents lived. I got a new sponsor, and she wanted me to "work the steps" all over again with her. Even though I'd already done them with my first sponsor, I agreed. We talked a few times a week, and my mother was often the topic. I still had some resentments toward her. As far as my family in general was concerned, a lot of resentments had vanished.

My sponsor suggested I do a "fourth step" just on my mother (see the appendix for a list of AA's and Al-Anon's 12 steps). Doing the fourth step means that you write down all the things you are angry or resentful about, and what you're fearful of, and how it affects you. Then you share this with someone you trust, and go through a process of trying to see where you may have been at fault and where you could forgive the other persons if they did something wrong.

I started writing things about my mother, and nothing was terribly new or dramatic. But one night I was thinking about her and I thought, "My God! What right do I have to sit around and pass judgment on my mother?" I suddenly saw myself, a thirty-something recovering alcoholic/addict/compulsive eater with no steady job and no husband and no prospect for either one. Just who did I think I was? I hadn't made much of my own life!

This was a tremendous realization for me, and immediately afterward I experienced a deep forgiveness toward my parents. I was suddenly more relaxed and wanted to be with them. This feeling has never left, and we are friends today. We don't get to spend a lot of time with one another, but the time we have together is very special.

Sarah—At Last

Sarah was the first of our children to be identified as an alcoholic, and she's the last to surrender finally to recovery. Her active alcoholism as we experienced it parallels the first sixteen years of my own sobriety. Though Dave and I have often felt whipsawed by the manifestations of her disease, Sarah has in retrospect been a powerful blessing. She compelled us to learn from Al-Anon and AA how to change ourselves to live with serenity and peace in the midst of anxiety and uproar. Her experiences have inadvertently benefited her brother and sisters, too. They saw what could happen to any one of them if they ever returned to drinking or using drugs. They also profited as Dave and I were able to apply our hard-won tools of recovery in relating to them.

During the recoveries I've recounted of the other three children, Sarah continued to drink. High drama, often involving hospital emergency rooms and sometimes the police, characterized her episodes. Dave and I gradually learned not to buy into the theatrical scenes of alcohol-fueled rage, recrimination, or self-pity.

When we first learned that Sarah might be an alcoholic, none of our family knew much about addictive disease. A confusing aspect for us was that she exhibited very different behaviors from mine. For one thing, she often preferred bars, whereas I stayed within my four walls and was drunk only among my family before I passed out each evening. Sarah rapidly developed into a far more public drunk, tending to become explosive and combative. Late one night, for instance, she nearly broke down the door at Rosie's apartment. Rosie's husband at the time, Jake, was understandably furious. He called the police. Sarah responded to the law by snapping off the antenna on the police car. In short order, the police subdued her and carted her away. Rosie believed her sister was going to jail, but instead the police delivered Sarah to the psych ward of the county hospital to dry out. Within twelve hours she had sobered up enough to talk her way out of the seventy-two-hour hold and return home.

Off and on, Sarah would go to AA and stay sober for a few weeks or months, once more than a year. During these sober intervals, she was a pleasure to have around. Then she'd relapse. It was hard for us to understand or accept, mostly because the rest of our family in recovery had never relapsed.

During my first year of alcohol recovery, I knew three or four persons who "slipped," and I agonized over their worsening conditions. I had little confidence that I could stay sober myself, but somehow I did. Just the thought of a relapse scared and kept me sober. A wise friend with twenty-five years of sobriety said that for some unknown reason, only about one-third of those who sought recovery remained clean and sober from the beginning. The other two-thirds would have one or more slips during the first year, but many of them were later able to avoid relapses. My friend emphasized that there was no moral difference between the two groups. People weren't "bad" when they relapsed, or "good" when they didn't. Just because you happened to fall into the one-third group didn't imply any kind of superiority.

In the mid-1970s and early 1980s there was still almost no solid information about "slips." Slips frightened other recovering alcoholics besides myself. "There but for the grace of God .....," we thought. At the same time, a certain stigma adhered to the relapser. "You must be doing something wrong," was the often unspoken criticism. Many times that was true. Alcoholics can be very pig-headed and self-willed. They may refuse to admit to themselves or anyone else that they need to pay attention to their recovery and not slide back into relationships, attitudes, or behaviors that can activate a compulsion to drink or use again.

I was fortunate to know a recovering alcoholic who was one of the earliest resources and researchers into slips. His interest and influence dated back to the 1940s. Every once in awhile I'd pick his brains. Later, as research and popular articles and books on relapse started to appear, I soaked them up avidly. They were very helpful in understanding Sarah's ups and downs. Quite early I learned the signs of relapse and the cognitive tools people could use to prevent slips, for myself as well as others.

Despite my best efforts I couldn't help worrying about Sarah's ultimate fate. Her drinking was so obviously violent. I could face almost anything except losing her forever through death. I dreaded getting a phone call that she was dead or maimed in an auto accident, or had killed someone else. I carried a secret I didn't dare vocalize for fear it would come true.

I believe in a God of love and compassionate justice, not a God of retribution and vengeance. Yet I couldn't help thinking that maybe our luck had run out with Sarah—that God (or karma, or fate, or whatever) would demand the life of one child for the three that were in recovery. I told no one. Then, when I was about six years sober, something happened that I can't explain. A dear friend phoned me out of the blue and said, "I've been reading something that may help you," and she read from her Bible. (In those preseminary days, the Bible was not one of my personal choices of resources, so my initial reaction was to humor my friend and listen politely.)

Matthew 18:12–14 (Jesus is speaking.) "What do you think? If a man owns a hundred sheep, and one of them wanders away, will he not leave the ninety-nine on the hills and go to look for the one that wandered off? If he finds it, I tell you the truth, he is happier about that one sheep than about the ninety-nine that did not wander off. In the same way your Father in heaven is not willing that any of these little ones should be lost."

How did my friend know the fear that gnawed way back in my mind? She didn't have any children, and had never even been married! Her intuition, so utterly on target, remains a mystery to me. I woke up the next day with the absolute conviction that the God of my understanding would take care of Sarah, no matter what. My anxiety about her dying collapsed. That possibility was still very real, but it was no longer my burden. I grieved at the thought of losing her, and knew I would mourn with all my soul if we did. The fear and anxiety were gone, though, and have never returned.

The irony was that at that time in my own recovery from alcoholism, I had no personal relationship with a Higher Power. I believed there was a God, or some kind of creative Power greater than myself. How else could I explain what I knew of our planet and solar system, to say nothing of the universe? As soon as I realized, however, that I totally accepted the existence of a Greater Power who was personally concerned with Sarah's welfare, I had to ask myself, "Why couldn't that be true for me, too?" From then on I began to know and appreciate what it meant to relate personally to

40

God. It was an unexpected and precious gift that Sarah unknowingly gave me.

Sarah kept plugging away in Colorado on her Ph.D. despite all the drinking setbacks. That she managed to succeed in such a demanding venture while continuing to ride the roller coaster of drinking and intermittent suicide attempts, is a tribute not only to her perseverance and stamina, but to a grace beyond her own strength. She was so volatile and unpredictable emotionally, however, that we were reluctant to have her visit us. In fact, we downright feared for our physical safety during one period. On one of her holidays at our apartment, we actually propped a chair against the inside of our bedroom door at night because there was no lock. Nor did we feel comfortable visiting her in her Colorado apartment. We didn't want *not* to see her, though, and were casting about for a way when my friend Hannah suggested meeting on neutral ground.

We had done a lot of camping with our children when they were growing up, so that's how we solved our dilemma. Each summer for five or so years we'd pick Sarah up in Colorado and go on a camping trip. One summer the three of us went to Europe. There were always difficulties, but we could keep them in better perspective away from our own turf. Sarah could explode or sulk and we didn't have to consider banishing her from our home. Dave and I were becoming more skilled at "detaching with love." We simply didn't get sucked into her emotional storms all that much anymore. There were many good times and happy memories, too.

In the mid-1980s, Sarah was awarded her Ph.D. with exceptional honors. She was immediately employed at a high salary by a leading computer company, where she stayed for seven years. Now, we thought, maybe she'll settle down and be healthy. Even with all our knowledge that new jobs or new locations would never "fix" an active alcoholic for long, Dave and I were still parents and wanted the best for our daughter.

Despite our hopes, Sarah continued drinking. After one especially severe binge she, for the first time, opted for hospital treatment, admitting herself to a thirty-day program similar to the one Rosie had gone through. Though Dave and I knew we mustn't project into the future, our hopes couldn't help but be raised yet again by this evidence of her independently seeking recovery.

It was Sarah's good fortune that the psychiatrist on duty at the alcohol and drug treatment unit was a specialist in addictive disease, who over the next several years would enable her to recognize and defuse a major source of her relapses, childhood sexual trauma. Sarah began to remember an episode, probably a series, of sexual abuse at the hands of teenage neighbor boys when she was only six years old. We never knew about it, for she was terrified they might kill us if she told. So she buried the memory, and whenever it threatened to surface, she would drink or become suicidal to blot it out. It wasn't the only trigger for drinking, but it was an important one. From at least adolescence, Sarah had classic but unidentified PTSD symptoms (post traumatic stress disorder) related to the sexual trauma: binge drinking, depression, emotional volatility, hypervigilance, a chronic inner rage, promiscuity, and obesity.

After discharge from the alcohol treatment program, Sarah resumed drinking periodically. She became increasingly unstable at times, and was often hospitalized as a psych patient for her own protection. Eventually, her work relationships were severely impacted and her employers fired her. It was the first in a series of hammer blows to her pride and sense of invincibility.

Dave and I were frightened both by Sarah's deteriorating health and by her loss of income, structure, and reputation. However, we tried to stay supportive as well as detached. The one consolation was her very generous severance package. We crossed our fingers and hoped she would find recovery before the money and health insurance ran out.

Just as her traumatic termination occurred, the PTSD climaxed with returning memory. She was virtually incapacitated by an inability to concentrate coupled with inner shakes and a kind of frozen numbness, and finally severe nightmares and frequent hypersensitivity to sound, light, and touch.

Sarah's emotional and physical states were so fragile, she could not live alone. On condition that she not drink, she returned to stay with us for a few months until she was stronger. We came to know firsthand how horrifying PTSD could be. I will never forget the many, many nights when Sarah fought sleep as long as she could for fear of the nightmares. Often I would be wakened by Sarah's screams and the awful trembling that wouldn't stop. All I could do was hold her in my arms and rock her like a little child. For the first time I had real compassion for her drinking relapses and binges. I could understand how a person might go to any lengths to avoid such pain and terror.

In my usual fashion, I turned to the growing literature on PTSD. Very soon I learned that a great many women in treatment for alcoholism and drug addiction have a history of sexual abuse. By now I was a chaplain in a large VA (Veterans Affairs) hospital. This hospital was a leader in treating war zone PTSD, first with men and then with women veterans. Nationally, the VA was also recognizing that the fallout from sexual abuse of women in the military was an important issue. It didn't take long for the VA to realize that the symptoms of war zone and sexual abuse traumas were virtually identical, and required a similar approach to treatment. Years before, I'd never have guessed that through Sarah's suffering I would be led some day to specialize in pastoral care of the sexually abused.

With care and patience her psychiatrist helped her through the acute stage of PTSD. She has vastly improved with treatment and time. However, PTSD of this intensity tends to remain chronic, and may reappear briefly and infrequently, though at far less damaging levels.

A symptom of sexual trauma is often obesity. Obesity is also a common stress response in family members of alcoholics. Until recent years, neither Dave nor I knew much about these connections. When Sarah was terminated from her job, she weighed 350 pounds. Dave was ashamed of Sarah's weight, but tactfully concealed his feelings. I've had a lifelong struggle with being overweight myself, though never to Sarah's extreme, so I felt more sympathy. I knew that obesity was usually the consequence of a very destructive addiction to food. We realized that Sarah's weight was truly pathological, but weren't fully aware yet of the connection to sexual trauma. We were very relieved when she began to shed pounds with the help of her internist.

A serious complication of the obesity was sleep apnea, a condition of interrupted breathing during sleep, usually accompanied by loud, persistent snoring. In Sarah's case, the apnea was caused by the diaphragm being pushed up against her respiratory system by all the excessive fatty tissue. The consequence of sleep apnea is sleep so frequently disturbed each night that the person is chronically tired the following day. As Sarah lost weight, the sleep apnea fortunately self-corrected.

However, there was one other complication of the obesity. It turned out that one of Sarah's antidepressants had a side effect of actually increasing her appetite enormously, thereby contributing to her weight gain. Even more critically, the medication drastically reduced REM sleep, a rare side effect. REM sleep is the intermittent dream state all humans need every night to remain balanced and rested during the day. The sleep apnea and the near absence of REM sleep were a potentially lethal combination—literally. Until the two conditions were corrected, Sarah routinely fell asleep many times daily from sheer sleep-deprived physical exhaustion—at work, at meals, on the highway, anywhere.

These particular complications of addictive disease and its treatment are mentioned here, not because they are typical of the addicted population as a whole, but because both short- and long-term complications of many kinds are typical in a proportion of those with addictive disease. It is not unusual to find two or more primary conditions coexisting; that is, addictive disease plus another primary diagnosis—what is called a "dual diagnosis." Clinical depression, a major primary diagnosis often related to a faulty body biochemistry, is fairly common in combination with addictive disease. Other primary diagnoses may involve the nervous system, the liver, the heart and circulatory system, and so on, and may either predate the addictive disease, be related to it, or develop independently. In any case, addictive disease only makes another coexisting primary condition worse.

In recent years, specialists in addictive disease have recognized that treatment for addictive disease may be unsuccessful if an accompanying primary diagnosis isn't also addressed. Thus the spread of dual diagnosis treatment programs which specialize in identifying and treating more than the addictive disease alone.

Finally, Sarah's acute PTSD symptoms subsided, her antidepressant was satisfactorily adjusted, and weight loss took care of the apnea. She was able to sleep through the night and wake refreshed. She resumed working as a consultant in her field, and we hoped she was through with the worst that could happen. It was not to be.

Just as Sarah seemed on a promising road to recovery, she resumed drinking and foolishly smoked her first crack pipe with a friend whom she had actually gone to help drive to a recovery house. Sarah was instantly addicted. We were stunned by the hair-trigger response of her system to crack. It took only that one initial hit of crack, and she was totally out of control. All those receptors in her brain went into overdrive.

The consequences were disastrous for her. In the space of six weeks, she lost her consulting contracts, went $50,000 into debt, sold furniture and numerous costly electronic items for a song, had no health insurance, and was in danger of losing her condo. By some miracle she still had her car. In four weeks she dropped twenty-five pounds, which she could actually afford to do since she then weighed between 250 and 300 pounds (but not that way nor that fast). The crack addict on a run has no time for eating or sleeping. Only the next hit matters. Sarah's fingers, lips, and mouth were grossly swollen and blistered from the extreme heat of the crack pipe and smoke. Her eyes were vacant. Her mind had gone elsewhere. She couldn't be reached.

Sarah couldn't have picked a worse time to go off the deep end. Trent, Rosie's husband, had just recently received what he had every reason to believe was his imminent death sentence from cancer. Not only were he and Rosie struggling with this tragic situation, the rest of our family was also in shock and grief. Now it seemed that Sarah, too, could die.

Once more money became an issue, as it often had in the past, though in a different context since Dave and I no longer regarded money as a symbolic expression of our personal power over anyone. Like many parents, we had gladly helped our children with the down payments on their homes. If Sarah defaulted on her mortgage, however, we would lose money we couldn't afford to lose as Dave approached retirement. So we stepped in and insisted that she rent out the condo and live somewhere else (not with us!) until she could get her life back together. She assented, and also gave her dad her power of attorney. That's how we became interim property managers in partnership with Sarah.

For several weeks, Sarah had some income from her last consulting contracts. Hoping she could stay clean and sober, Dave and I lent her the small balance she needed to live in a series of halfway houses for a few months. Then one afternoon we returned from a weekend trip to find our apartment had been burglarized. Sarah had stolen the VCR to trade for crack, and one of her "friends" (suppliers) had returned on his own and taken a lot of jewelry, Dave's expensive tools, and assorted other items. Most of all we mourned the loss of irreplaceable family heirlooms such as Dave's grandfather's gold watch, and unique jewelry I had inherited from my mother and treasured in her memory.

I think I knew all along at some level that this might happen. Goodness knows we'd heard plenty of similar examples in our years in AA and Al-Anon. Dave and I immediately called the police and filed charges. Surprisingly, perhaps, neither of us was angry. Our response was instead a profoundly sad but unequivocal, realistic acceptance that we had to take such a step. We would have done the same with anyone who burglarized us. We had to assume that her crack addiction could impel her to additional transgressions against us. We changed the locks on our door. We notified our apartment managers that she wasn't to be given access to our unit at any time. We cut off all the slight remaining financial support and refused to feed Sarah or allow her in the apartment.

From our years in Al-Anon, we found the strength, courage, and amazing serenity that comes only through a deep trust in a God of mercy and compassion, as well as of justice. We knew we had to stand aside and let our child become totally homeless and penniless, hungry and without food, ill, living on the streets, in her car, and in our urban ministry's church shelters—hostage to the legal system and the courts.

Sarah was shocked to her toes by what she had done, and by the inexorable consequences. One of the most honest and up-front persons alive, she was appalled and deeply ashamed to have resorted to stealing. Without question we had her attention. On top of Dave's and my reaction, the rest of the family—Andy and Karen, Susan and Alex, and Rosie and Trent—were simultaneously terrified and furious. Unwilling and/or unable to handle this new escalation in Sarah's addiction, each one promptly cut off all communication with her in order to lessen their own pain and fear. Devoted to her siblings and their spouses, Sarah was crushed. Andy and Karen also forbade Sarah to contact their daughter, Ann, who was the apple of Sarah's eye. This was a particularly bitter pill for her to swallow.

Those early weeks were a very hard time for Dave and me. We understood and empathized with the rest of our family, but in the beginning we felt great sorrow at this desperate rending of the kinship fabric. We ourselves had no intention of denying all contact with Sarah, though we would certainly limit it more than we ever had. Neither were we going to rescue her in any way. She needed to live with the consequences of her actions.

Sarah pleaded guilty to a felony. Since it was a first offense, she was given three years' probation instead of a two-year jail term. For three months she was homeless, living in the church shelters. Having no job, she hung out in AA meetings, where her friends often supplied her with cigarettes and would sometimes give her a little money for a haircut or something extra. The next six months she was in a court-ordered women's recovery home, in which AA attendance was mandatory. After that she lived in a series of ever nicer rooming houses, culminating for eighteen months in a pleasant cottage of her own. Somehow she managed to stay clean and sober.

We will always be grateful for the steady support and understanding in our recovery communities. The "outside" world can be very judgmental about parents like us. From strangers I literally heard the words, "How can you refuse to feed your daughter? For shame!" Sometimes it was hard not to be judgmental about ourselves, and instead keep hands off except for providing encouragement and hope.

Sarah's physical and emotional health was so impaired by crack in the beginning, there was no way she could resume work for almost a year and a half. During that time she immersed herself in AA. She went on disability, and managed thereby to pay her own expenses. Even though it hurt her pride, she was also grateful. This cushion was a blessing while she needed it.

Sarah couldn't trust herself not to spend her money instantly for crack. Dave agreed to handle her finances in consultation with her until she felt able again. Her main concern was to keep a barrier between her crack compulsions and immediate gratification. Sarah told her dad what to write the checks for, including her own spending money. I privately worried sometimes that she might take $20 in cash and blow it on crack, but Dave serenely and without any questions did what she asked. It wasn't easy over the next two years for Dave to walk that tightrope, but he did it fairly and with flair. What a difference in his attitude toward money from seventeen years earlier!

One particular friend has shepherded Sarah through recovery from the ravages of crack. Margo, who'd had her own battles with crack and alcohol several years before, told Sarah she was one of the angriest people Margo had ever met. She was right, but we in the family had become accustomed to the two-by-four, not just a simple chip, that Sarah carried around on her shoulder. It took an outsider to challenge her. Every day Sarah was required to write down all her resentments and fears and read them to Margo over the phone. Gradually over the space of a year, most of Sarah's anger was dissipated. Margo was her faithful coach and friend. It's difficult to overemphasize the impact of this development in Sarah's recovery. The defusing of her core of rage has had wonderful healing effects on everyone around her.

It goes without saying that Sarah's psychiatrist and internist were equally important in the healing process. They've stuck with her for years, through all the hard times. Dave and I do not share some of the common fear and disdain of drugs in the treatment of conditions that may accompany addiction, providing the need is medically demonstrable, the physician is truly knowledgeable, and the client is a responsible partner. Unfortunately, a blanket judgment against all drugs, of any kind, at any time, is sometimes apparent in the recovery communities. This backlash happened to Sarah, creating extra conflict and distress for her. Periodically, she tries reducing or eliminating a medication, only to regress into depression or early PTSD symptoms. Dave and I worked patiently to keep reassuring her that in taking her prescribed medications, she was not a failure choosing the "easier, softer way," but rather an intelligent, brave woman willing to go to any lengths to maintain her sobriety, her sanity, and her life.

A valuable lesson I finally learned was that I didn't have to be the family information center. Our children had somewhat come to expect that even if they didn't communicate with one another at times, I'd always have the latest news to pass on. Actually, I thought that was one of a mother's important jobs—to keep everybody informed. When Sarah's siblings closed their own doors against her, I decided it wasn't in my job description after all to be communication central, and so informed everyone. No more secondhand news. If they wanted to know what each other was doing, they'd have to pick up the phone themselves.

Dave never was one to gossip, but he didn't go to my extremes of not sharing any news, so a little information leaked through. Andy, Susan, and Rosie continued their normal frequent contact with one another and with Dave and me. Dave and I maintained communication with Sarah. As time passed, however, I could see that Sarah's siblings were as hungry for news of her as she was of them. It was difficult for me to abide by my decision, but I did. Now it seems natural, and far healthier, to leave control of their own intercommunication to our adult children, and not feel any responsibility for it.

It would be months before Andy and then Rosie warily reopened their lines to Sarah. Susan took longer. Today communication is fully restored among them. Sarah is now also reconnected with her in-laws, Karen, Trent, and Alex. As Sarah demonstrated how serious she was about her recovery, Dave and I slowly relaxed our earlier prohibitions. At first we didn't want her in our apartment at all. In a few weeks, we were cautiously comfortable with having her visit as long as one of us was here. When she continued to recover after a year had passed, we felt justified in giving her a key again. Now while we're away, she takes care of the plants and mail. She currently eats most of her dinners with us, and shares the cooking. We enjoy having her back in our lives.

At the end of eighteen months, Sarah was reenergized and increasingly healthy. She returned to work as a full-time, self-employed contractor. She had continued to lose weight, and was then about 220 pounds. A cigarette smoker from early adolescence, she decided to quit her two-pack-a-day habit. Our other three children had given up tobacco years earlier, but Sarah couldn't seem to despite many attempts. The nicotine patch, nicorette gum, and joining Nicotine Anonymous (a 12-step support group for nicotine addicts) have all been a big help. For the first time since she started smoking as a teenager, she's been free of cigarettes for more than just a few days, since fall 1994. As parents, we're as grateful for recovery from this ferocious drug as we are for the arresting of her alcohol, crack, and food addictions. Her asthma vanished. And contrary to her fears about not smoking, Sarah kept losing weight slowly. When she broke 200, she had a party.

We've been very fortunate in having good tenants for Sarah's condo. She is steadily repaying her debts and straightening out her financial affairs. When she celebrated her second clean and sober anniversary, she felt able to resume full control of her money. Within a few days she decided that she wasn't quite ready when the crack compulsion resurfaced after being dormant for many months. These powerful flashbacks are common the first few years for recovering crack and cocaine addicts, and can easily be triggered by ready access to money.

Sarah celebrated her third clean and sober anniversary by moving back to her condo. The whole unit was scrubbed from top to bottom, and completely repainted for the first time in seven or eight years. Sarah had new carpeting installed throughout. Two new sofas replace the ones she sold to the last tenants. She plans to have a house blessing in a few weeks when the refurnishing is complete.

As it turns out, that traumatic day in July 1993 when we had Sarah arrested became the wonderful first day of her new life. She's been clean and sober ever since. We couldn't know that at the time, however. All we could do was practice the solid principles we had learned in Al-Anon and AA, and trust that the God of our understanding would do for her what Sarah, and we, were unable to do.

No one knows what the future holds for any of us, certainly not for Sarah. We can only pray that she stays healthy, ever evolving into the beautiful soul that was always there.

Sarah's Story

I began my drinking and drugging career at the age of thirteen. I loved the effect both alcohol and drugs had on the way I felt, though alcohol was my favorite. LSD and marijuana scared me many times. In college I didn't drink much during the academic year, but I went nuts sexually and with alcohol in the summers. During my last semester at college, I started bar drinking again.

After college I moved to Chicago and worked as a computer programmer. I began doing really crazy things, like drinking windshield wiper fluid and ending up in the hospital while in an alcoholic blackout. When I returned to California I drove a cab. I felt so proud and relieved because I wasn't drinking every day—some days I'd just be too hungover and too sick to drink!

I drank and gambled my way across Nevada en route to graduate school in Colorado. In Colorado I frequently got drunk, making late-night calls to my family and friends, and cutting my wrists and threatening suicide. Cutting my wrists minimized the emotional pain, making me feel real because physical pain was concrete and simple.

My mom, at this point, had started going to AA. I tried it my first year of graduate school, but only lasted a few weeks without a drink and then I started all over again. Mostly I was a bar drinker because I liked to be around people. Over the next few years, I tried AA off and on, but never managed to stay sober permanently.

While in Colorado, I became addicted to cocaine and went downhill very fast, spending thousands of dollars I didn't have on the drug. Later, while living in the San Francisco Bay Area, I discovered crack. I sold most of my valuable belongings and risked my life in crack houses and with crack addicts. I was in and out of several county shelters and recovery homes for addicts.

The start of my last drunk was helping myself to my father's liquor when my parents were out of town. I went on a five-day bender. Twice in that short period I took an overdose of pills and ended up as an indigent in the county hospital. We slept on plastic couch pillows on the floor—no blankets or privacy.

Somehow, I got ahold of $20 and took off on a crack binge. Since I'd already sold all my own stuff for crack, I stole my parents' VCR, thinking I'd somehow redeem it before they returned. I don't remember much after that until the next morning when I came to in a crack house without my car keys and wearing someone else's shirt. Apparently I had puked all over myself. My fellow crack addicts had cleaned me up and changed my shirt, but I have no memory of all that.

I knew that one of the men had probably taken my car and burglarized my parents' apartment using my keys. Finally, he returned and I got the car keys back. At that moment, I surrendered. I felt so low. In the afternoon my friend Margo met me at a coffee shop. My mother was there. She told me I was being charged with grand theft, and confiscated my keys to the apartment.

The three of us went to the apartment. My father had called the police, who read me my rights. I was charged with first-degree burglary, a felony. However, instead of jailing me after fingerprinting, etc., the police released me to my parents' custody for a few days until I detoxed.

Then I was out on my own, with no money and no place to live. I tried living in my car for one night, but it was very scary. The worst part was going hungry. Finally, I realized I had no choice but a homeless shelter, where I stayed for three months. After that I was in a court-ordered women's transition house for six months.

Since the night of the burglary nearly three years ago, I've been clean and sober. I believe that I finally hit my bottom when I stole from my parents. This, and all the other things I did on that last time out, were just too much for me. I shall never be able to repay my parents for everything taken. It's something I shall have to live with. I will also have to live with the knowledge (gained in sobriety) of how I hurt and terrified my parents, my brother, and my sisters.

I owe a lot to my psychiatrist of eleven years. In his office, we've discovered that I suffered a severe sexual trauma at the age of six when our family lived in Hawaii. In the safety of his office, I've encountered those demons. It's been very hard, but well worth it.

I've learned much about living sober from my sponsor. She's a great source of hope and encouragement. With her I've shared thoughts that I would not be able to share with anyone else. And she still accepts me, loves me, and thanks me for trusting her.

I quit smoking in the fall of 1994, have been employed for eighteen months, and have lost 160 pounds. I take care of myself by exercising daily and eating a balanced, nutritious diet. I haven't cut my wrists in years. I am very reliant on my alcohol and nicotine recovery groups.

I have a Higher Power to whom I pray, and turn my will and life over, on a daily basis. God has worked miracles in my life. My belief stems from the utter desperation I felt when I hit bottom with alcohol and crack. I believe I'm a better person today. I love people and try to be cheerful and caring with those I meet. Life is very valuable and fragile. I especially like reaching out to newcomers in the recovery groups, and carrying my message of experience, strength, and hope.

The Open End

For a few years while I was busy studying and commuting to seminary, both Dave and I dropped out of Al-Anon, except for occasional visits. However, we continued consciously to recall and practice the valuable tools we'd learned. We had found and integrated a new way of life. When Sarah collapsed with crack, however, we immediately fled back to Al-Anon. In our fear, we badly needed its reassurance, hope, and stabilizing influence. We share our own experience, strength, and resurgent hope freely with others.

In our meetings we've been reminded that denial is a hallmark of both the alcoholic/addict and of those around them. Dave and I were so naive and so blind that we totally missed the developing disease of addiction in our teenagers. All we saw were the behavioral problems. We attributed those to adolescent growing pains. Later, when our children were adults, we tended to prefer our image of what we wished them to be, and thus discounted any evidence to the contrary until circumstances and growing knowledge forced us to open our eyes.

Some of that knowledge concerned the prevalence of polyaddiction. Dave and I are of the generation that essentially knew only one addictive drug, alcohol. Today it is unusual to meet an addict who uses a single drug, though he/she may prefer one among several. Our children have been among Dave's and my most important teachers in this respect.

Nor did Dave and I at first have any sense of how either a parent's or a child's active alcoholism could complicate and skew a family's dynamics. We now have absolutely no doubt that alcoholism and addiction affect not only the person afflicted, but everyone around them as well. To survive in this kind of stressful environment, outside support from others in comparable situations is a great advantage. We have come to value deeply and appreciate the power in the combined wisdom of people who've had experiences similar to ours.

What we subsequently learned from family systems theory, and experienced for ourselves, was that when one person began to get well, the family relationships would probably get much rougher for awhile before they settled into a new stability. A support community for the family at these times can be critical. It surely was for Dave and me as each of our children found recovery in very different ways. Adjusting to a sober family member may be as problematic as coping with the drinking consequences.

As parents of alcoholics, Dave and I also realized over the years how important it is to adhere to basic principles of healthful living in order to reduce stress, even when we didn't feel like it: exercise, adequate rest, and balanced nutrition. To these we added prayer and meditation. In our experience, these five principles are not only good common sense, they're indispensable preventives of otherwise seemingly unmanageable stress.

Both of us regard meditation simply as sufficient physical relaxation to clear and empty the mind for a short period. It's a relief to know how to shut off the worry. Prayer has come less easily. However, necessity can be the mother of invention. There's much to be said for "Help!" and "Thank you" addressed to God. The Serenity Prayer remains basic. We've learned to listen as well as direct our thoughts in prayer. Today we also find strength and support in the church to which we returned after a long absence.

Detaching with love

We don't have any magic formula for mastering how to "detach with love." My first lesson in this crucial principle came shortly after Sarah moved to Colorado. Dave and I were still at the beginning of our understanding of what it means to be the parents of a child with addictive disease. One morning Sarah phoned and said, "I'll be on the noon plane. Please have someone meet me." Immediately, our anxiety gauge zoomed up.

"What's the matter?" we asked.

She wouldn't say. Our imaginations took off. We feared the worst, whatever it was. Luckily an out-of-state friend, who had a couple of alcoholic adult children herself, happened to be visiting with us for a few days. I was afraid for Sarah, but also resentful for letting myself be manipulated by her. Yet I remember crying out to my friend, "Why can't I be a better mother and welcome my daughter?" My friend gently but firmly directed our attention to the fact that an adult child's life and decisions were not our responsibility. Moreover, if this peremptory phone call had come from just a friend, we might have said we'd love to see the person, but it wasn't possible to pick her up or have her stay with us at this time since we already had a full house with another guest. In other words, while adult children, even sick ones, should be treated with courtesy and concern, it's not necessary to subjugate our whole lives to their every whim.

Sarah was very drunk when she arrived. Her impetuous trip was the result of an alcoholic's typically impulsive behavior. When she sobered up in a day or two, she flew back to school in Colorado.

Detaching with love is a process, like learning to ride a bike. You practice and practice, fall down and get up, try different speeds, and test the brakes—and one day you realize you've got the hang of it. It's an exhilarating feeling of freedom from bondage—the bondage of old fears, old attitudes, and old behaviors. It's the freedom to enter into and enjoy healthy relationships with oneself and others, and freedom for a healthy spirit of cooperation with a Greater Power, who will at times do for us what we cannot do for ourselves.

Joy and Fun

One of the most important discoveries Dave and I have made in our recoveries as parents is refinding a sense of joy and the ability to have fun—two of the most important parts of recovery. Developing these qualities in the midst of chaos takes both practice and perseverance, but it can be done.

Together Dave and I have developed a common passion for opera, birding, travel, and music—I have the broader tastes in music, while Dave rarely strays from the classical. We each have a couple of personal major interests; for Dave it's genealogy and working on cars. My lifelong avocation has been dance of all kinds, both performing and teaching. I am an insatiable reader, and in the last fifteen years, I have become addicted to crossword puzzles. As we renewed or added these activities in our lives, we found they were a major help in sustaining us even when life seemed bleakest. I can't overemphasize how greatly our lives have been enriched by these activities. Instead of spinning faster and faster into a vortex of fear and obsession around our children's addictive disease, where we had no time or energy for ourselves, we have been released to the deep refreshment of the spririt that comes through recreative activities. We enjoy each other's company as well as our many social contacts. And we enjoy our children, too.

It is always a critical sign of health and sanity when recovering parents can genuinely laugh and enjoy themselves and life.

Conclusion

Perhaps the central lesson Dave and I have integrated is that neither of us is God, nor is any human being. Instead, we have experienced an awesome Power greater than ourselves, both in our own lives and in the lives of our children. This belief has been of utmost importance in addressing the issues of control and expectations.

The illusion of control is very seductive. Like anyone, Dave and I have considerable control in choosing our individual actions, thoughts, and feelings, but very little—if any—over another person or events. Yet we by no means give up on spheres of influence outside ourselves, for we firmly believe in the power of the individual to influence others at least through example. Groups of like-minded individuals can certainly effect change in systems.

The line between "letting go" and not taking action is a fine one. Intervention with Rosie would have been impossible had we adhered to the extreme of no action whatsoever. On the other hand, we no longer spend our energies trying to compel others to our control. It hasn't been easy to let go of expectations, either—especially for me. Though experience may sometimes suggest probable results of certain actions, we know now that we definitely don't have the power to predict outcomes with absolute certainty. In adult human relations, there's also no way to control the outcomes. We can surely hope, but too often we've been either happily surprised or been found wrong. Dignified, honest humility through trust in a Higher Power has proven to be a strength, not a weakness.

It's hard not to succumb to black-and-white thinking in reacting to alcoholics, yet we've learned never to say "never." Instead we try to be fair to ourselves as well as others. The role of doormat doesn't appeal, nor does permanent rejection, especially if the person is sincerely trying. We also remember that addiction is truly a disease often characterized by relapse, so we're realistic as well as hopeful about the future for any one of our children. Like parents of children who have other chronic, potentially fatal, diseases, we're thankful when our children are in remission and recovery. We know that today is the only day we, and they, can ever really count on.

We are also very mindful that in one important sense alcoholism and drug addiction are far from the worst chronic diseases our children could have. Addictive disease can be held in complete remission and the person fully restored to normal functioning. By contrast, in other chronic diseases there may be neither cure nor remission, and little hope of resuming total function. Dave and I know that for Andy, Susan, Sarah, and Rosie, their disease can be permanently arrested, and they themselves continue to be completely restored to vibrant, joyous health.

"Gratitude" is the word that best describes how Dave and I feel about what's happened to our children and to us. In December 1994, we celebrated fifty years of marriage. That's a miracle in itself, considering the obstacles my alcoholism raised. An equally great wonder is how our children and their spouses came together in love for us and one another, to give us a beautiful party we'll always treasure in our memories. Just a year before, the family was torn apart in anguish by Sarah's crack use. Fear, anger, and estrangement were rampant among her siblings. The reunion of our children since then has been no flash in the pan. Dave and I see a deeper bonding and appreciation for one another, and for the fragility of life.

Following the anniversary gala, Dave and I left immediately for three grand weeks of a second honeymoon in Costa Rica, where we spent Christmas and New Year's. This was the first time we hadn't been at home with our family for the holidays. It felt a little odd, but also very liberating—and lots of fun!

This has been the story of two parents of children with addictive disease. It's a somewhat unusual story because all four children are alcoholic/addicts, and because the six of us, including the one non-alcoholic, Dave, are in recovery. We've described affairs from our own perspective as parents, which will differ from the perspectives of our son and daughters.

Sometimes Rosie, Dave, and I tell our stories before a community or church group. People are fascinated to hear about the same events as seen through the eyes of the child of an alcoholic, the spouse of an alcoholic, and an alcoholic (in this case, me). But Dave and I have never told our complete story as parents of alcoholics. We hope this account will help other parents in some way. As they say in Al-Anon and AA, however, "Take what you like and leave the rest!"

Our hearts are full. Each of our beloved children has already been blessed with God's grace and healing power. Dave and I can ask no greater gift.

PART II
THE NATURE
OF THE DISEASE

One of the very first steps parents can take is to become informed about addictive disease. What is it, and how do you know if someone has it?

Imagine Such a Disease

If some new and terrible disease were suddenly to strike us here in America—a disease of unknown cause, possibly due to noxious gas or poison in our soil, air, or water—it would be treated as a national emergency, with our whole citizenry uniting as a man to fight it.

Let us suppose the disease to have so harmful an effect on the nervous system that 6½ million people in our country would go insane for periods lasting from a few hours to weeks or months and recurring repetitively over periods ranging from 15 to 30 years.

Let us further suppose that during these spells of insanity, acts of so destructive a nature would be committed that the material and spiritual lives of whole families would be in jeopardy, with a resultant 25 million persons cruelly affected. Work in business, industry, professions, and factories would be crippled, sabotaged, or left undone. And each year more than one and one-quarter billion dollars would need to be spent merely to patch up in some small way the effects of the disease on families whose breadwinners have been stricken.

Finally, let us imagine this poison or disease to have the peculiar property of so altering a person's judgment, so brainwashing him that he would be unable to see that he had become ill at all; actually so perverting and so distorting his view of life that he would wish with all his might to go on being ill.

Such an emergency would unquestionably be classed as a countrywide disaster, and billions of dollars and thousands of scientists would be put to work to find the cause of the disease, to treat its victims, and to prevent its spread.

The dread disease envisioned above is actually here. It is alcoholism.[1]

Ruth Fox, M.D.
*President, American Medical
Society on Alcoholism*

---

1. From *Marty Mann Answers Your Questions About Drinking and Alcoholism,* © 1970 by Marty Mann. Reprinted by permission of Henry Holt & Co., Inc.

Addictive Disease

A Public Health Issue

Addictive disease is America's most serious public health problem. No other disease afflicts as many persons. No other disease approaches its impact on individuals, families, the health care system, businesses, and the economy. It is estimated that at *least* five persons are directly affected by one person's addictive disease. No other disease contributes to as many deaths directly or indirectly (for example, auto accidents). No other disease bleeds the economy, private and public, like this one. We may think that addictive disease is a private, personal matter, but in truth it contaminates all areas of society. Dr. Fox's passionate statement which introduces this chapter was written in 1969 about alcoholics but is applicable to the whole of addictive disease.

Moreover, the disease has a strange mirrorlike effect on persons close to the one afflicted. Many *nonalcoholic* parents will see themselves in some of Dr. Fox's passages. We have heard the story of a man who held a responsible professional position in a large company. His colleagues noticed first that he was becoming somewhat careless in his dress and grooming. He began to call in sick on Mondays. Then he would take Friday and other days off, too. He lost weight. His eyes were bloodshot, his face puffy. Sometimes he forgot to shave. His personality changed from easygoing to short-tempered and volatile. His job performance deteriorated drastically.

This company had educated its supervisory staff to recognize some classic physical and secondary behavioral signs of alcoholism like the ones just described. After a couple of warnings to shape up, the man's manager one day confronted and fired him for incompetence due to alcoholism. The man turned around and sued the company for defamation of character. He was a lifelong teetotaling Mormon, and indeed had never touched alcohol or any other drug. Instead, his *wife* was severely ill with alcoholism, a fact he was desperately ashamed of and had tried to keep secret.

For a year the man had exhausted himself caring for his children and his home all by himself, in addition to attempting to control his wife's drinking. His eyes were red from sleepless nights spent waiting up for her to come home in the wee hours. He was burning himself out, and still his wife continued her downward slide. Until he was fired, he did not recognize how irrational his own behavior had become, and the degree to which he mirrored many of his alcoholic wife's symptoms—without any alcohol in his system.

Before World War II, addictive disease was generally considered a moral issue. Religious and ethical norms labeled the addict a sinner. This was understandable since the behaviors of alcoholics and addicts were frequently immoral—from chronic lying, petty theft, and abdication of responsibility, to adultery, domestic violence, and major felonies. But poor morals are not the cause of addictive disease. Instead, they are typically the result.

This is not to say that the addict's behavior should be excused. Most parents understand, however, how to differentiate between a child's act of wrongdoing and the child himself, between an *illness* and the *person* who is sick. Once the individual has stopped drinking and using, it is essential to continuing recovery that moral behavior commence, including restitution for the past, or the person is in danger of relapsing.

Definition of Addictive Disease

This book considers addictive disease only in connection with psychoactive drugs. A psychoactive drug is one that affects the mind or central nervous system. Alcohol is a psychoactive drug, so *alcoholism* and *drug addiction* are interchangeable terms.

Not all psychoactive drugs lead to addiction. For example, most of the psychoactive drugs used by psychiatrists are not addictive. However, it is always prudent for an alcoholic or addict to discuss and periodically review a proposed medication of any kind with the attending physician. Maintaining personal secrecy and anonymity with one's doctor in this case may be hazardous, even life-threatening.

In addictive disease, how the drug is ingested doesn't matter, whether by drinking, smoking, in a pill, via a needle, or whatever. It may be noted in passing that related manifestations of addictive disease such as compulsive sex, compulsive overeating, and compulsive gambling exhibit patterns very similar to those in the following definition.

> *[Addiction is] a disease process characterized by the continued use of a specific psychoactive substance despite physical, psychological, or social harm.*[2]

Richard B. Seymour and David E. Smith, M.D. describe addiction as "a disease entity with its own psychopathology characterized by compulsion, loss of control, and continued use in spite of adverse consequences. Addiction is progressive, potentially fatal if untreated, and incurable but remissable through abstinence and recovery."[3]

Addictive disease is a primary disease in its own right. It has a unique, distinctive symptomology and progression. It is not the consequence of another disease, nor is it caused by an underlying psychological or personality disorder. All sorts of personalities become alcoholics and addicts. Physical and mental disorders, however, can coexist independently with addictive disease.

When we think of *disease*, we usually have in mind germs—bacteria and viruses. But there are many conditions commonly called diseases, such as diabetes, that are not caused by germs or viruses but by malfunction of some part of the body. In the case of diabetes, the pancreas malfunctions. Some diseases have genetic causes, such as sickle-cell anemia. Still others can be traced to the environment, as in lead poisoning.

Another group of diseases seems to have both genetic and environmental or sociocultural components. Such appears to be the case with addictive disease. In the individual with genetic and sociocultural vulnerabilities, the potential for addictive disease is greater. However, this disease will not be activated unless the individual ingests a psychoactive drug.

---

2. American Society of Addiction Medicine.
3. Seymour and Smith. *DRUGFREE*.

Genetic Factors

The specific gene or gene sequence has yet to be identified in addictive disease, but the disease definitely has a powerful physiological, apparently inheritable component. Also, while a gene or genes for addictive disease may be inherited, there also seems to be a possibility that the disease can be triggered in some persons by repeated use of a psychoactive drug without any familial history of addictive disease. For instance, regular, but initially not compulsive, drinking of alcohol, especially in larger amounts, may permanently shift certain persons into the compulsive, addictive mode.

Sociocultural Factors

Sociocultural factors include family customs and behaviors, peer pressure, work and recreational patterns, and so on. Though a personality disorder does not *cause* addictive disease, the initial indulgence in a psychoactive substance may be launched by a person's immaturity and sense of unease in a given setting. Most people, for instance, often drink a beer or glass of wine to relax in a social situation. Because the potential addict appears at first to respond within a normal range to common sociocultural stresses, the disease can be difficult to diagnose in its early stages.

Especially in the case of adolescents and young adults, "getting high" may be viewed merely as a temporary rite of passage prevalent in American culture. Many recovering alcoholics who come from families severely affected by a parent's alcoholism say they swore they'd never be "like that." But peer pressure in adolescence may start them down the path despite their best intentions. Later on, at-risk young adults who also want to fit in may believe they have the maturity and good sense to know when to stop.

Psychoactive Drugs

There are many psychoactive drugs, legal and illegal. The two drugs that activate most of the addictive disease in the United States are nicotine and alcohol, both of them legal for adults and both by far the most widely used. Nicotine may be the most addictive substance known. Nearly everyone who starts smoking becomes addicted, often right away. All the illegal "street" drugs put together come in a distant second to alcohol and tobacco, both in usage and in effects on society. Yet street drugs tend to capture the greatest political and media attention.

Note that most of the drugs mentioned in the following brief outline have honorable and well-established legal medical uses. Only when the psychoactive drug is used without informed medical supervision does a problem arise. Psychoactive drugs may be classified in a number of ways. The following classification is based on material from the Haight Ashbury Free Medical Clinics of San Francisco, one of the country's leading treatment and research centers for addictive disease.[4] Under each category are listed some typical, common examples of drugs.

Narcotics and Analgesics

These are the opiates, including morphine, codeine, and heroin. Withdrawal may be uncomfortable but usually not life-threatening. Overdose may be fatal.

Central Nervous System (CNS) Depressants

These are the sedative-hypnotics, including alcohol, barbiturates (sleeping medications) such as Seconal, and benzodiazepines (tranquilizers) such as Valium. Withdrawal may be painful but is not life-threatening. Overdose can be fatal.

Central Nervous System (CNS) Stimulants

These are the "uppers," including cocaine, crack, amphetamines, and caffeine. (Nicotine is both a stimulant and a depressant.) Withdrawal may be so upsetting that the individual has great difficulty in stopping use of the drug. Caffeine overdoses are rarely life-threatening, but cocaine, crack, and amphetamine overdoses are—in addition to inducing severe, suicidal depression on withdrawal.

Psychedelics and Hallucinogenics

These include marijuana, peyote, LSD, and psilocybin mushrooms. Withdrawal reactions vary with the individual and the

---

4. Seymour and Smith. *DRUGFREE.*

dosage, and may be prolonged over several months. Depression severe enough to be life-threatening may occur. Overdoses may be extremely life-threatening because in a resultant psychotic state the individual can lose contact with reality and disregard personal safety, for example by jumping out of a window in the conviction that he/she can fly.

How Do Psychoactive Drugs Work?

The brain has different receptor sites for specific classes of drugs. A receptor site is like a keyhole awaiting a particular key to unlock it. An opiate—one of the morphine derivatives, for instance—is commonly administered after surgery to reduce pain and facilitate healing. Opiate receptors in the brain lock onto the morphine and the drug reduces sensations of physical pain and anxiety.

Receptors function through the brain's neurochemistry, which contains pleasure circuits as part of every human's genetic inheritance. Psychoactive drugs are not the only stimulators of these pleasure circuits. The brain itself can produce natural nondrug "highs" in several ways: by aerobic exercise, meditation, good food, sex, stimulating companionship, mastering a skill, making a discovery, and the artistic creative process. The lure of psychoactive drugs is that they are stronger, quicker, and more reliable in affecting the pleasure circuits. Receptors aren't selective. They welcome any kind of input from their specific class of drugs, whether oral, injected, or through the lungs. It should be noted that the brain does not contain receptor sites for alcohol. Instead, the body's biochemical systems are deranged.

Among addicts, polyaddiction is common, that is, addiction to more than one category of drug. Most addicts quickly learn through experience how to mix and match or substitute drugs as available and preferred. A recovering alcoholic says she found that she had a certain level of "drug hunger" that kept growing over time. She could fill it up with alcohol on some days, with cocaine on other days, with Valium sometimes, and so on. Usually, though, her personal preference was about half alcohol, half cocaine on any given day. The cocaine (a stimulant) jazzed her up; the alcohol (a depressant) brought her down. Unfortunately, her receptors for cocaine then began to demand ever more attention, followed by cries from her biochemical system for increased alcohol. The total she needed steadily grew. A proverbial "vicious cycle" took over, resulting in the need for more and more alcohol and cocaine to satisfy her hunger.

Demographics of Addictive Disease

Addictive disease knows no boundaries. It is endemic throughout the world. People of every race are susceptible. In the United States, the commonly accepted incidence of 10 percent of the population is probably too low, but no one knows for sure. Estimates run as high as 25 percent.

All ages are represented, and age of onset runs the gamut from in utero to very old. Infants with addicted mothers can be born physiologically addicted themselves. "Crack babies" are heartbreaking examples. There is reason to believe that ingestion of *any* psychoactive substance during pregnancy, including nicotine, may adversely affect the fetus. The younger the person, the more acute the disease often seems to be, and the faster the progression.

Neither intelligence, education, income, living conditions, nor social status are protections against the disease if the genetically vulnerable individual continues to ingest a psychoactive substance. Addictive disease is thoroughly democratic. "Silk sheet" addicts are as common as "skid row" ones. The former simply may not be as visible because they're typically protected by their families and their money.

Intervention

As addictive disease progresses, all kinds of crises begin to escalate in the addict's life: family crises, work crises, legal crises, and health crises. These become increasingly severe. They occur more often, and start to overlap in time. The recovery communities describe the process as a down escalator that ends in death or a permanently damaged brain. Each lower step on the escalator is a crisis. Sometimes, if the addict is lucky, one or another crisis will tumble him or her from the downward slide with sufficient force to stay off and start the climb back into recovery. Threat of a job loss, or the actual loss, is a pivotal crisis that can motivate an addicted person to seek recovery, or the threat or actual loss of a child and/or family may do so.

Experience has shown that intervention (see glossary) can interrupt the inexorable journey on the down escalator and facilitate recovery from the disease. Briefly, such an intervention has three essential components:

- A counselor professionally trained in the intervention process for addictive disease, who coaches the interveners in the preparation and procedure, and conducts the intervention session.
- A united front by the designated interveners (usually family members), meeting as a group for the intervention session.
- Strict secrecy from the intervenee by the interveners until the actual intervention starts.

For a thorough discussion of how this kind of intervention should be designed and implemented, refer to *I'll Quit Tomorrow— A Practical Guide to Alcoholism Treatment* (see appendix). Also, see pp. 23-25 for our family's experience of a professional intervention with an addicted child.

Adult Children of Alcoholics

The damage to children growing up in a home where one or both parents have addictive disease is well documented. Therefore, parents who are themselves adult children of alcoholics (ACA) may have unknowingly developed childhood patterns of responding to addictive disease that are not useful in relating to addictive disease in their own children. Common among parents who are ACAs are excessive fear, an extreme obsession to control and "fix it," and unresolved ancient angers. Such parents seem to have a particularly hard time recognizing the limitations of their individual human power in addressing addictive disease in a child.

Today there are numerous resources for adult children of alcoholics. Many ACAs find it helpful to attend groups especially for them. The resources in part 4 provide a good introduction to the organizations and literature that are available.

Violence, Domestic and Otherwise

Domestic Violence

Domestic violence is violence that occurs in private homes. It is a repetitive learned behavior. Its purpose is to establish and maintain power and control over another person, yet the perpetrator is unable to maintain internal power and control over him or herself. Psychoactive drugs do not cause violence, but by lowering or removing inhibitions, they add fuel to a fire that's already smoldering.

Nearly always, the perpetrator of domestic violence is related to, or close to, the victim—not a stranger. Nothing the victim says or does, or fails to say or do, will change the perpetrator's cycle of violence. However, there are specific, crucial methods of ensuring safety for a victim. Please see the resource section.

Domestic violence takes several forms—emotional, verbal, physical, and sexual. Both sexes are guilty of emotional and verbal domestic violence, but females are more likely to exhibit these forms of violence. In physical and sexual violence the perpetrator is often a man, the victim a female or a child. The high incidence in the United States of domestic *physical* violence alone—once every six seconds against a woman—is one of our country's tragic secrets.

Parents of children with addictive disease may find themselves the object of emotional, verbal, and physical violence from their children. Parents may also be the perpetrators of violence against their children, particularly when the children are smaller and can't fight back. Parents of actively alcoholic and addicted children often report their dismay and shame at having used the weapons of emotional and verbal violence in futile efforts to control the disease in their children. Various studies in treatment centers for addictive disease indicate that as many as 90 percent of addicted women also have a history of sexual trauma, usually perpetrated originally by a male family member.

Public Violence

Public violence is more readily recognized than domestic violence. American society seems very aware of violent public crime and the need to do something about it. Often not realized, however, is that many violent public crimes occur under the influence of a psychoactive drug, commonly alcohol. Several studies indicate that anywhere from 50 to 70 percent of prisoners in local, state, and federal jails and prisons may have addictive disease. Many parents of addicted children already know firsthand about sons and daughters who end up incarcerated.

A thorough discussion of domestic and public violence is beyond the scope of this book. However, more and more information is available today from public and private community resources that address this issue. Parents of children with addictive disease can benefit from learning about the scourge of violence and its relation to alcohol and drugs.

Specialists in Addictive Disease

Today an important new medical specialty exists, *addiction medicine*. Addiction medicine is now recognized by the American Medical Association as a distinct specialty. Addictionologists are physicians and other health professionals who specialize in treating addictive disease. They undergo special training and certification in addition to their medical degrees. Some addictionologists may specialize further in treating adolescents or women. Wherever possible, addictionologists are the preferred practitioners in the treatment of addictive disease. A noncertified practitioner should at the very least be thoroughly up-to-date in the pharmacology and treatment of addictive disease.

Treatment

Treatment for addictive disease begins with diagnosis and intervention, followed by detox, stabilization, and a long convalescence. There is no known cure. Abstinence is considered the only proven basis for permanent recovery. Modern treatment protocols include early identification and treatment of coexisting primary diseases or conditions, for example, severe clinical depression or liver disease.

Experience shows that abstinence is easier to maintain if the person makes changes in behaviors and attitudes that will support an abstinent lifestyle. For many people, this means more or less continuous long-term outside help and encouragement, often provided at virtually no cost through self-help groups.

At present, treatment programs for addictive disease are again undergoing drastic realignment as they have in the past.

Because alcoholism and drug addiction were not widely recognized as legitimate diseases until well after World War II, medical treatment was not generally available except for brief hospital detoxification as needed, or in case of an acute life-threatening situation. Medical personnel, in fact, preferred not to encounter alcoholics and addicts. These patients never seemed to be cured. They rotated in and out of the hospital, and were notorious for not paying their bills.

In the meantime, Alcoholics Anonymous, founded in 1935, began to have success in arresting the disease with some significant fraction of those alcoholics who tried that approach. The Hazelden Foundation in Minnesota then developed a residential treatment program that combined a medical model with the 12 steps of AA. This became known as the Minnesota Model of Recovery, and was widely duplicated throughout the United States during the 1970s. The usual treatment pattern was about thirty days of intensive inpatient care, followed by a year or more of outpatient aftercare. One size fit all. Today, with increased understanding of how psychoactive drugs work in the body, length of treatment tends to be individualized as much as possible.

Because comprehensive private health insurance coverage for treatment of addictive disease was fairly available until recent years, hospital-based treatment programs proliferated. In addition, counties and other local jurisdictions developed public programs to address the needs of citizens without private insurance. The 12-step programs (for example AA, Cocaine Anonymous, and Narcotics Anonymous), which had for many years been the primary recovery resources beginning with the detox stage, increasingly concentrated on the long-term recovery of the individual and had less to do with the first few weeks.

The treatment picture is changing again as private insurance coverage in this period of transition in health care is drastically reduced or eliminated for hospital-based inpatient programs for addictive disease. Even outpatient treatment is feeling the pinch. At the same time that private insurance for addictive disease is diminishing, so is public funding for county and other local treatment programs. Once more the 12-step and other self-help groups will probably find themselves in demand to respond to the individual in the earliest stages of detox and recovery.

These developments are complicated by the prevalence of polyaddiction and dual diagnoses (see glossary), which often require medical attention that the 12-step programs are not qualified to provide. In addition, while the behavioral and attitudinal changes suggested in the self-help programs are generally psychologically sound, the spiritual thrust of some of them does not appeal to everyone. Part 4 includes organizations and readings that address such issues.

Convalescence

Recovery from addictive disease usually has a long convalescent period. While detox from alcohol may last only a few days, complete detox from other drugs may continue for weeks or months. After the detox stage, it is not unusual for the individual recovering from psychoactive drugs, including alcohol, to take a year or more fully healing physically, and another year or two becoming emotionally stable.

Parents may be fooled by the child's increasingly healthy outer appearance. The physical inner damage done by psychoactive drugs to nerves, organs, tissues, biochemical balances, and so on, is repaired gradually. Given enough time, the body eventually will find a new, healthy equilibrium that leads to a positive, optimistic outcome for permanent recovery.

Recovery is hastened and strengthened by a well-rounded diet that is low in refined sugars (skip the sweets and junk food!), plenty of exercise and fresh air, daily relaxation, adequate sleep, no caffeine, and withdrawal from nicotine as soon as possible. These guidelines work as well for us parents in restoring our own equilibrium as for our children recovering from addictive disease.

Also recommended early in convalescence are thorough medical and dental exams. Such checkups are routine in hospital-based treatment programs, but they're equally important in every convalescent setting so that any deficiencies due to addictive disease or masked by it, may be identified and addressed.

Relapse, especially during the first year of recovery, is not uncommon, frightening though it may be to hopeful parents. In fact, addictive disease is presently considered a disease in which periodic relapse may be as characteristic as permanent abstinence. A realistic fear, of course, is that recovery from relapse is unpredictable. Will the person even live? How many others may be accidentally killed or maimed?

Banishment of a relapser from treatment programs used to be the only response. Today, some programs instead recognize the need to encourage the relapser to pick him or herself up and stay in treatment. This has always been the approach of Alcoholics Anonymous and its sister 12-step programs. They say, "Keep coming back!" and "Bring the body; the mind will follow."

What Can We Do?

First and foremost, **remember that addiction is a *disease*.** You didn't cause it, you can't control it, and you can't cure it. That said, there's a lot we *can* do, for ourselves and for others. The stories in this book are full of healthful, sensible, practical ideas you can apply to your own life and situation.

How to address the huge personal and public health issues of addictive disease is complex, but researchers and practitioners already know many pieces of the puzzle. Their experience strongly suggests that several commonsense approaches need to be implemented as a package. Individual parents can do a great deal for themselves and their children, but there is strength in numbers. Private and public resources are also essential.

What Parents Can Do

Get Help for Yourself We parents need help as much as our children do. Fear, isolation, worry, and exhaustion will make us sick and our addicted children worse. Our nonaddicted children and other family members will also suffer if we don't find help for ourselves.

Take Care of Yourself Eat well. Rest well. Play well. Practice letting go. HALT is a good acronym to remember: Don't get too Hungry, Angry, Lonely, or Tired. It is not selfish to care for oneself. It makes good sense.

Find a Support Group for Yourself Find a group that is knowledgeable about addictive disease. Our peers are invaluable guides and teachers. Al-Anon has a long, distinguished record of helping families and friends of alcoholics. Some areas of the country offer special Al-Anon groups for parents (and grandparents) of children with addictive disease.

Talk to an Addictionologist or Therapist

Talk with someone who specializes in addictive disease and in the treatment of parents as well.

Learn as Much as You Can About the Disease

We wouldn't hesitate to consult with all the resources we could find if our child had diabetes, cancer, a developmental disorder, or asthma.

Educate Yourself

Find out about the relation of addictive disease to other problems, such as crime, domestic violence, school dropouts, malnutrition, births out of wedlock, and HIV/AIDS, to name a few.

Take a Look at Your Own Use of Alcohol and Drugs

This includes nicotine and prescription drugs. Outside opinions from family, friends, and coworkers can help you decide if you need to change in this respect.

Take an Honest Look at Your Own Use of Any Form of Violence (verbal, emotional, physical, or sexual)

Get help for yourself if you need it.

What Society Can Do

We parents need all the help we can get. Both private and public resources are necessary to address the larger societal issues related to addictive disease. It's up to us to demand these resources, for the sake of all our children and for the benefits to society itself.

Education

Education about the disease should begin in kindergarten, and continue through high school. Included should be constantly updated education of parents, teachers, school administrators, and school counselors. Treatment professionals need better education. Medical schools, for instance, are by and large seriously deficient in educating about addictive disease. Finally, an informed media can be instrumental in ongoing education of the public at large.

Counseling

We need counselors and therapists trained to respond with the very best information and help about addictive disease. We need them in schools, in business, in churches, and in the community.

Intervention   For the individual addict, this resource should be activated at much earlier stages of addictive disease, before the person lands in prison, is permanently disabled, or dies. In the case of societal intervention, we need to continue effective local policing and international drug interdiction. We also need to direct attention to interdiction of *domestically*-produced psychoactive drugs. Americans are the largest growers and distributors of marijuana to our own citizens. The recent rise in adolescent consumption of marijuana has its source in the great marijuana "ranches" out in our country's hinterlands. Domestic advertising of alcohol and tobacco products probably does even more harm.

Treatment   Although we can reduce the incidence and severity of addictive disease for many people by following the first three steps above, the disease will always be with us. Adequate treatment should be assured to all who need it, including the large numbers of addicted persons currently incarcerated. Use of treatment for addictive disease should be a regular part of the criminal justice system. In addition, treatment should incorporate what has been learned about the special needs of adolescents, women, and older adults.

Punishment   This is an option of last resort, but one that society chooses most often because of failure to provide the far less costly preceding four options. A recent very large definitive study in California under the leadership of Andrew Mecca, Director of California's Department of Alcohol and Drug Programs, demonstrates convincingly that punishment costs seven times as much as prevention and treatment.[5] Punishment alone also generally decreases motivation for recovery from addictive disease.

Important Corollary Steps   The five steps above outline society's major responsibilities in addressing addictive disease. In addition, practitioners in the field have learned that a successful approach should include attention to some or all of the following: schooling, jobs, housing, child care, transportation, parenting skills, nutrition and legal services.

---

5. *Evaluating Recovery Services: The California Drug and Alcohol Treatment Assessment* (CalData). General Report Publication No. ADP 940-629. Dept. of Alcohol and Drug Programs. Sacramento, CA. August 1994.

Conclusion

Clearly, addictive disease is no simple matter. It cannot be addressed in a vacuum, emphasizing one approach at the expense of others. The personal and public aspects of the disease are intertwined. There are many steps parents can take to help themselves. There are many steps the addict can take. There are many steps that we need our voluntary and treatment communities, and our local, state, and federal governments and agencies to help us with.

Read the stories in this book. They will give you hope, courage, and strength. Start using the resources that are available to you. There *is* life at the end of the tunnel!

PART III
OTHER PARENTS
TELL THEIR
STORIES

Parents themselves should not *abuse* alcohol and drugs, including nicotine and prescription drugs. The parents in these stories either never have or are no longer doing so. While it is possible to start making changes in one's other life behaviors and attitudes, a parent's own reliance on alcohol or drugs will severely curtail personal progress toward serenity and wholeness. In addition, children are vastly more influenced by what parents do than by what they say.

Coming to Terms with a Daughter's Disease

A Father's Story

My daughter, Marie, was born an addict. When my wife and I took her home from the hospital at the age of two days, we had no idea her genetic mother suffered from the disease of alcoholism/addiction.

A year later my wife's gynecologist informed us that the mother had another baby on the way, and asked if we'd like to adopt our second child. Our son, Aaron, was born free of the disease.

The early years of our family went well. I was a happy and proud father, and I believe my wife was also happy. Then everything started to fall apart. Our marriage ended, we sold our home, and my wife moved a thousand miles away, taking the children with her. I visited them as often as I could. Before long, Marie was telling me how they were being ignored and physically abused. I was ignorant of the severity of the situation, or in denial because I had no way of facing the truth. Just before Christmas of 1971, when Marie and Aaron were ten and nine, their mother packed their belongings and told them to leave. I was off the next morning to gather my children and bring them home.

The effect of being abandoned, first by her genetic and then by her adoptive mother, and of being ignored and abused and made to feel worthless, along with her predisposition toward narcotics, proved to be more than Marie could handle. Before long I would find alcohol in her room, then marijuana. I remained somehow oblivious to the seriousness of my daughter's condition, attempting to manage with no parenting skills whatsoever. I had been raised by an emotionally disturbed mother and a father who wasn't there for us. I do not offer this as an excuse; a part of me still feels that my inability to give my daughter the nurturing she needed was as instrumental as any of the other factors that led to her addiction. All I could give her was love, and that wasn't enough.

My son was a quiet child who didn't seem affected by all that had happened in his young life. Instead of acting out his hurt, he held it in. Today he is a respected teacher, married to a wonderful woman who also teaches, with a beautiful daughter and a son on the way. However, "the body can't be deceived; it knows our true story very precisely,"[1] and Aaron suffers from numerous chronic physical ailments, manifestations of his inner pain.

Marie dropped out of school and went out on her own at age sixteen. She stayed close to home and would come back to live for short periods of time. Her daughter was born in 1983, and her love for Jeanette seemed for awhile to diminish her need for drugs. But before long drugs were again a part of her life.

Marie moved with her baby to a city a hundred miles away. We'd talk on the phone, and I'd drive up for visits. I knew she still had a drug problem, but my ignorance and denial kept me from understanding its severity. In early 1988, my daughter told me she was a herion addict. I spent the next eight months trying to find help for her, with no idea where to look. My son and his wife had persuaded Marie to let them care for her child. My daughter's drug abuse increased, and our lives were filled with anxiety and despair. With the help of my nephew, a recovery home was found, and Marie agreed to enter. It was to be the first of four recovery periods and six homes over the next eight years. Her longest period of sobriety lasted three years. Her first recovery attempt led to my becoming a grateful member of Al-Anon.

Shortly before Christmas of 1988, I visited my daughter at her second recovery home. She had been there a month, as a follow-up to her initial thirty day program. We were sitting on a park bench when she told me how glad she was to be an alcoholic, because it gave her a family that would always be there for her wherever she was and whenever she needed them. I remember feeling absolutely certain that her days of drug use were over, but within the next few months she had slipped, and by early fall had lost custody of her six-year old daughter and was out on the streets, heavily addicted to heroin.

I'd see or hear from Marie occasionally over the next twelve months, but it would invariably end in angry words and threats of suicide. I was waking in the middle of the night sweating and shaking. Our family doctor, fearing suicide on my part, started me on

---

1. *The Drama of the Gifted Child.* Alice Miller. Basic Books, Inc. New York, NY. 1981.

antidepressants, which subdued the physical symptoms and kept me numb but able to function. They did not keep me from feeling responsible for every bad thing that had happened, and I knew it was up to me to provide a cure for Marie. I was attending Al-Anon meetings regularly, but wasn't really getting the message. However, I did keep coming back; I had nothing else. One of the things I kept hearing was, "Don't quit before the miracle."

While all this was going on, Jeanette was being cared for by her father and his mother. Though the bond between Marie and her daughter was strong, the years of confusion caused by drugs had taken its toll. Jeanette was out of control. In seeking help for my granddaughter, I was put in contact with an old friend I hadn't seen or heard from for twenty years. In those ensuing years she had become a child therapist, and Jeanette and her father started attending weekly sessions that quickly led to her recovery.

In October of 1990, I was about to leave on a long-anticipated vacation when I was notified that Marie was in jail for drug possession. She wanted me to bail her out, but through the miracle of the program I was able to say no. She had met my friend Francine, who was counseling her daughter and was also involved with a women's recovery home. I reminded her of this, and told her I loved her and had complete faith in her recovery. When I returned, she was the loving daughter I had remembered, two weeks into a recovery that would last three years.

Sometime in late 1993, my daughter experienced physical problems which led to an addiction to pain pills. A year passed before the old addictions took over, but she managed to stay close to AA and have brief periods of sobriety. In March of 1995, Marie agreed to enter into recovery close to her home, so she would have a support group nearby. She stayed for over five months, and then relapsed. Another fall and winter of drug use, with short periods of sobriety, followed. In March of 1996, Marie reentered the home, and again, after a five month stay, relapsed. I do not consider any of this to have been a mistake or a failure. Marie's ultimate recovery is just taking longer than I expected. I've always had unreasonable expectations; I think that's what kept me going, and kept me falling.

As I write this, it's almost Christmas 1996. My daughter appears to be clean again. I don't really ask; I love her and accept her just as she is, in or out of her disease. I'll be leaving tomorrow to spend Christmas Eve with Marie and her partner, and Christmas Day with Aaron and his family.

We hear that addiction is a family disease, how it reaches out to affect all members of the family. Aaron detaches (if it's with love, he keeps it inside) and will have nothing to do with his sister when she is in her disease, or for awhile after. Their mother, who has come back into their lives, also coldly detaches. I no longer try to bring them together. Al-Anon and my blundering actions over the past eight years have shown me that any intercession on my part is counterproductive. My love for my children and grandchildren is constant and equal, but I can no longer survive feeling their pain and knowing there is nothing I can do to help. I work the program around all facets of my life, and now feel free from the pain of others.

What brought me this freedom? I'd thought I had the Al-Anon message immediately: I was not responsible for Marie's addiction. I did not cause it and I could not cure it. All I could do was keep the focus on my life, and trust that my daughter's Higher Power would keep her from harm and one day return her to a safe and sober life, to the spiritual person she had always been.

I went to meetings and read the literature. I talked the talk but was unable to walk the walk. Somehow the part about getting a sponsor and working the steps eluded me. On the Friday evening before Christmas of 1995, I walked into an Al-Anon meeting and heard a very spiritual man tell his story. It was my story, even though he had no children and later told me he wondered how he could possibly help me. Stan told me to read Step 1 (see appendix)[2], and to call him when I returned from my Christmas visit with my children.

I left the next morning to spend a few days, and Christmas Eve, with Marie and her partner. The next day we drove to my son's home to celebrate Christmas Day. It was a "let's just pretend everything is fine" time, but on the drive home I realized that my daughter was in her disease, and that I was powerless and my life had become unmanageable. The first step was easy.

The God of my childhood was a vengeful, judgmental God, and it was very difficult for me to come to believe that a Power greater than myself could restore me to sanity. Stan said to fire that God, and to write a want ad for a loving God:

_____

2. *Twelve Steps and Twelve Traditions*. Alcoholics Anonymous World Services, Inc. New York. 1953.

WANTED: HIGHER POWER

You must deliver me from my need
to feel in charge, to control.
You must free me from my obsessions.
You must be able to pull me out of
any depression, and release me
from the anxieties that drain me.
You must show me my God.
You must help me see my Daughter
as a good soul put on earth
by God to work out her own salvation.
You must help me to see
the good in everyone. I will
call upon you night and day, so you must
be available at all times. I will settle
for less at the moment, but you must
have the potential to accomplish
all of the above.

Turning my will and my life over proved even more difficult. I'd never had anyone to turn anything over to, had always felt the need to do everything myself, and had believed that God the Avenger was not on my side.

But I remembered, "Don't quit before the miracle." I didn't, and one evening, when everything seemed hopeless, I went to bed with what seemed to be the deepest heartache I'd ever known. In desperation I "turned it over" and fell asleep. When I woke the next morning I remembered what I had done, but I could not—and to this day cannot—remember what had troubled me. My new God had not only taken my grief away, but left me with no remembrance of it. I still see this as a pure miracle.

Steps four through nine showed me what working the steps really meant. Making a searching and fearless moral inventory of myself meant not only finding my part in all the resentments that had built up, especially within the family, but also discovering that, besides being a blundering codependent, I was also a caring and loving father who did all he could to help his children. I forgave others, but more importantly I forgave myself. I wrote about my fears, and they were many. I admitted the nature of my wrongs to this new God of mine (I'm still agnostic, but miracles speak louder than reason), to myself, and to my sponsor. It was a little like going to confession as a child, but Stan attached no guilt nor penance to my thoughts and actions as the priest had done. I felt no more guilt, and my fears disappeared.

Step six meant making a list of my shortcomings. These character defects were survival techniques I had learned from my childhood and early adult life. I was now ready to face and accept life on its own terms, and set about ridding myself of them. I wrote about my pride, and learned humility. As I asked God to remove my shortcomings, they fell away. No miracles here, this is everyday work. Sainthood still eludes me.

I made amends. The most dramatic of these were to my son and his wife, whose lives had been most affected by my attitudes and actions. Since Aaron and Ann lived close to Marie, I had expected them to keep an eye on her and be there to pick her up whenever she fell. They were doing graduate work and starting their teaching careers, so my demands were putting a big strain on their marriage. I hope that my amends lifted the curtain of hurt and resentment that had come between us. I like to think that when I told my son, "You are a good person. I love you and accept you just as you are," I freed him from feelings of insecurity about himself and anger toward me. What I know is that these amends freed me from my feelings of guilt over my past actions. I also felt a great freedom in knowing that I had no power over the lives of others, and with this sense of freedom came a release from my codependent behavior.

I'm now working and practicing the so-called maintenance steps, promptly admitting my wrongs when they come up, meditating to set my mind free, and praying only for the grace to accept the will of this Power that has proven to be greater than any I could have imagined having within me. Step twelve is next, but I already find myself practicing these principles in my life. Carrying this message to others is tricky. I have nothing of the preacher in me, and those who know me would be turned off by any display of righteousness. I feel a sense of freedom from the self I've lived with all my life. If I have a message, it will show itself silently.

At Thanksgiving of 1995, I stayed with Marie while she was detoxing from a short period of drug use. I wrote this poem the next morning, while she slept.

THE DAY AFTER THANKSGIVING

I'm at my daughter's home—she's slept twelve hours now.
They say it's the recovering that does it, the body's need
to feel safe, unexposed. I hold with that, but worry...

It's what I do. I laugh at myself. I flow with gratitude
because she's cared for, and not left alone
to fight her dragons. When she wakes

I'll ask if we might go to the river, idle the afternoon
sitting on the bank watching the gulls and mallards
rise from their danger, circle around

in the air that shelters them, then settle back in the river
to drift on the current that moves them
safely each day of their lives.

I came to terms with my daughter's disease by accepting her just
as she is, a beautiful person created by God, born with an affliction
through which she and I, and those close to her, might learn more
about ourselves and the value of unconditional love and acceptance.

Now when you ask me, "How's Marie?" I say, "I don't know, ask
her." Ask me how I'm doing and I say, "Some days are great, and some
days are better." As it says on page 88 of of the Big Book,[3] "It works."

3. *Alcoholics Anonymous, Third Edition.* Alcoholics Anonymous World Services, Inc.
New York City. 1976.

From Hard Scrabble to Serenity

Teamwork Pays Off

Catherine: We first noticed Earl had a problem with alcohol and drugs when he was a high-school freshman. I was called to the school because he was cutting classes. When I asked Earl where he'd been, he said he was out in the back of the school.

Vern: In the beginning, we didn't know about the alcohol and drugs. What we saw was his behavior. To support his habit he stole from us and others. I was pretty free with my money to Earl. It was an easy way for him to buy all the drugs he wanted to use, because Dad would readily shell out the money.

Catherine: In March of his sophomore year, Earl was picked up for shoplifting. On the day scheduled for the juvenile parole hearing, he was dressed and ready to go when suddenly he freaked out and refused to leave the house. He was high on amphetamines and became so agitated that he stormed out the door. I couldn't reach his parole officer, so I phoned the police for help. When Earl came back inside, he said he was going to mimic having a gun so the police would shoot him.

I called the police back and told them, "Be careful. He's not really armed."

When the police arrived, they talked to him. Earl admitted he was depressed, so he was taken to the county hospital emergency room for evaluation. In the end, he was referred to a forty-five-day 12-step residential treatment program for adolescents. All three of us had to be interviewed before the program accepted him. Vern and I were required to attend parents' meetings twice a week and also go to 12-step beginners' programs (both Al-Anon and AA).

Vern: In the first group session for families, each kid had to tell how much alcohol and what drugs he or she had used, and in what combination. Some teenagers were dealers, thirteen- and fourteen-year-olds! Earl admitted he was smoking sixty marijuana joints a day, using crank, drinking alcohol, and doing several other drugs as well. It was quite an eye-opener.

Catherine: Earl was in treatment only thirty days when he was suddenly terminated and had to come home. We were in a panic. We were totally unprepared.

I've been very fortunate that Vern and I have worked together, in combination. We've tackled this family problem together. We both began going to Al-Anon. From another couple we heard about a particular Al-Anon group called Parents Letting Go. There we learned that Al-Anon was for *our* healing. We were part of the problem and it was for us to get our act together. Basically, that meant to get out of Earl's way. At the same time, we tried to make a contract and force him into NA (Narcotics Anonymous) programs.

By the end of the first six months, we realized that we couldn't force any intervention on him. If he wanted to make progress in his own recovery, that was up to him. We would have to get out of the way and let him fall on his face, if that's what it took. So we stopped searching for the marijuana pipes and the drugs. We stopped questioning his behavior.

Earl had come out of the treatment program at the end of April. By June—between missing school while in treatment, having cut classes during the year, smoking and drinking alcohol on the school grounds, and being suspended for smoking pot at school—he had missed virtually his whole sophomore year. I tried to sign him up for summer school, but he lasted only two days.

What did work was an alternative type of school. In the beginning it was bumpy. The school had my beeper number and they would tell me Earl had cut classes. Later Vern and I would talk with Earl about it.

Gradually, as Vern and I stopped our frenzied behavior and the searching and questioning, Earl's attitude started to change. He settled down in school. He went more frequently. Earl has special education needs. He's dyslexic. He should wear glasses, which he refuses to do. And he did start changing some of his friends. Actually he was going back to a few of his old, better friends, which was amazing. In the recovery programs, alcoholics and addicts learn they've got to get away from the old crowd they've been involved with. Slowly we saw improvements.

The one piece of literature that I found the most important for myself was the Alcoholic's Letter to Loved Ones (page iii). The letter was very powerful. After reading it, I realized addiction is a disease. A person with addictive disease is more to be pitied than crucified.

The daily meditation book, *Courage to Change*, was my bible the first six months. When something would hit with Earl, such as his cutting school, I would say the Serenity Prayer like a mantra. I would just say it over and over to get control of myself. If I found myself depressed or fearful or angry, I'd go back to that book and read the relevant sections.

The name of our Al-Anon group, Parents Letting Go, was also very powerful for me. From the beginning I instinctively knew I had to let go. In trying to intervene or solve Earl's problem, I was somehow an impediment. I needed help in learning how to let go. I've found a lot of encouragement in Parents Letting Go. The name is so right.

Vern and I joined a second group, Nar-Anon, which was more oriented to the families of narcotics addicts. Because there were often stories about teenagers, it was easier for me, personally, to relate to. I find great comfort in Nar-Anon.

Even after a year and a half, I continue to go to my recovery meetings because they refocus and balance me. I realize there's no instant cure, and the meetings keep me on the right track. Though I've heard many of the stories many times, I hear them from new perspectives as I myself grow and change.

I've found that I can use the program in other aspects of my life—for example, with colleagues at work. I need to think before I talk, especially with Earl. It's so hard to do that, and it's so easy to slip back into old ways.

Vern: My story is different from Catherine's. We're both voluminous readers, but when it comes to the recovery program and working the 12 steps, I can't get into reading the material. That doesn't work for me. I'm sure there are many people, particularly men, who are in the same boat. We don't want to read, but we do want to learn. I'm more of a listener.

When I got into the program, I knew things had to change. I didn't know who had to change or what had to change, but I knew things had to change. Now, after a year and a half in the program, I realize that the addict has to change, the parents have to change (if it's a parent-child situation), and *both* parents have to change. A 12-step recovery program provides the structure. I can refer back to the steps and say, "I haven't done this yet," or "I haven't done it well enough yet," or "I haven't done it recently enough." I can remind myself what I still need to accomplish in order to have serenity.

The whole goal is my serenity. It's not anybody else's serenity, it's mine. I like to think of the 12-step program as a sieve. You put in everything you have when you come into the program—the good and the bad. Hopefully, only the good comes through, and all the bad is left behind. Of course, we know that's not true; some of the bad does leak through. Maybe you have to sieve again and again, until you get it right.

Catherine: Recently, I've had to practice "detachment with love," a concept we're learning in Al-Anon. Earl accumulated some traffic tickets from speeding on his moped, riding without a helmet, and so on. For awhile he worked to pay off the fines. Then he lost his job and was coming up to the deadline for paying off the tickets. He needed to go down to the court to get an extension. Instead of driving Earl to court and negotiating with the judge myself, I gave Earl money for the bus and told him how to get to court. He actually did it.

Vern: Earl chooses not to attend a 12-step recovery program, but while he was in treatment he learned some tools that help him. He understands and tolerates Catherine's and my regular attendance in a 12-step program of our own. He knows he can still push certain of our buttons, but in other ways that doesn't work anymore.

As a result, we're now approached differently in some instances. If Earl wants money, he doesn't just say, "Man, I need money to go skating." If he wants money for skating, he has to be explicit. He has to outline and specify the request because I don't buy off on any old story and Catherine doesn't, either. Consequently, he's much less demanding in what he requests of us.

Al-Anon has taught us to say, "Hey, we want to set some boundaries here. We know we can't control you 100 percent with the money we give you—you might use it for something else. But we're going to require a commitment. Either you'll use the money for what you say you will, or you're going to lie to us. If you lie to us, we have a breakdown of trust. Trust is the only thing that keeps the family together."

One of the issues we've had is driving the car. Earl is now seventeen and will be eighteen in about six months. He does not drive. The reason he doesn't is that Earl and I have an agreement that when he can come and tell me he's been clean and sober for thirty days, then I will allow him to go ahead and get his driver's permit and I will put him on my insurance policy.

This has been our arrangement for a year and a half now, and Earl has never come up to me and said, "I've been clean and sober for thirty days. Let's go get my license." Therefore it's an unstated fact that he's not yet been clean and sober for thirty days. Because he's worked very hard at being frank with me during this period of time, I have to accept that he's telling me the truth.

Truth is a bond on both parts, on the addict's part and on the parent's part. The other night I asked Earl, "Have you been using? You look like you were." Earl answered, "Well no, not drugs. I had some drinks." So, we have the ability to communicate honestly if I ask him what he's done. He doesn't tell me if I don't ask him. And I don't try to pry unless I think it's an issue that should be raised.

When we first came into the program, I'd just go nuts if Earl told me he'd used. Now if he tells me, I don't go nuts because I understand that he has a problem. I'd rather he be honest with me so that we can work out a solution together.

Many times he's been using marijuana, and in his mind that's not an issue. "That's not abuse. It's not drug use," he claims. I can't change his ideas about marijuana, yet he knows that I don't care for that type of conduct. I accept that he wants to use, but we do have boundaries.

Another boundary with Earl is that he can't sneak out at night to go use. Many boundaries are unstated, though. They're inherent in the family relationship, and concern pride of family and common standards of conduct in our society. These unstated limits are in a gray area. Our understanding and tolerance changes with our learning curve in the 12 steps. We may see that we can't control some of these issues after all. Then we can let go of the frustration.

Catherine: You can also let go of resentment. In many cases, kids have stolen money and other valuables from their parents. Last winter Earl stole something very valuable to me. I decided the resentment wasn't worth holding on to. It was only because of the fellowship program that I was able to do this. I would probably be resenting it to this day, and that's a big waste of energy.

Vern: A big issue for parents with teenagers is the financial liability. We can't control the addict and we can't control the addict's behavior. The only chance we have of influencing an addict's behavior is to get out of the way and improve ourselves so the addict can make some progress. In the meantime, the addict may come into conflict with the law, and encounter situations that make us financially responsible. It's always, always on our minds.

Catherine: Times like this, you don't give the kid a car. I've seen friends make the mistake of doing that over and over again.

Vern: That doesn't mean a kid won't steal or borrow a car or, like my son did, take his moped and go out riding without a helmet, a driver's license, or any insurance. Earl did the same thing twice, within about a week. The first time cost him $150; the second time, $350. He paid off the first fine and most of the second one before the deadline. The judge said the $350 was because Earl didn't have enough common sense to go get a driver's license. Earl told the judge that he couldn't get a driver's license because he had a contract with me that he couldn't get his license until he stopped using. The judge wasn't real fond of hearing that, but he did allow him another sixty days to take care of the fine. How Earl will handle it, I don't know. It's his problem. He's got to pay it. That's part of his growing up.

Catherine: I don't drive Earl to school anymore, either. He has a monthly bus ticket. It's his responsibility to get himself to school. It's up to him to get out of bed on time and go to bed on time. He complied fairly well. I stopped hauling his body all over town. You know, "Mom, take me here. Mom, take me there." That's just ridiculous and I won't do it. Because of our change of attitudes, we don't have the verbal and physical violence we once had.

Vern: Earl and I have had several physical altercations, but not once has either of us hit the other. I remember particularly the last time my son and I fought. Earl and Catherine were arguing. I thought something was going to occur so I stepped in between, right in his face. Earl got two hands on my chest and pushed real hard. It knocked me back.

I got mad and went after Earl because I felt he was attacking me personally. It turned into hard scrabble. I hurt my thumb down on the floor. Finally I had to tell Earl to let me up. At this point, I basically told my son, "That's it with physical confrontation. We aren't going to do this anymore. If we can't discuss issues, then we need to find other ways to solve our problems. Our relationship is too valuable for us to just throw away because we want to prove who's the best man."

He agreed. We made a verbal bond at that moment, even though we were still trying to calm down. Despite Earl's problems with drugs and despite our resistance to that issue, we have a good healthy love for each other. That was a year and a half ago. Earl still uses, but fortunately much less, I think. We're all able to focus better, he as an individual, and Catherine and I as a team, so that we can continue as a family.

Catherine: I think the word "team" needs to be underscored. As parents, we have to be on the same page. It was hard for Vern to attend the midafternoon meetings at Earl's treatment center. He had to take off work. He really put out the extra effort to get to those meetings.

We go as a team to Al-Anon and Nar-Anon. Even though we work our programs at different levels, we're still on the same page with Earl. Our expectations are the same and the limitations we set are the same. We think that's extremely important. Single parents have a very hard time. Even in a divorce situation where there's a common child, a team effort is essential. I can't think of anything more chaotic than the husband and wife pulling at each other on top of it all.

Vern: I'd appeal to all the guys that aren't supporting their wives in a recovery program. This business of being so macho that you don't have to go to these kinds of programs, you don't have to do the book work, you don't have to do the study, you don't have to do the reflecting and changing, because you're the man of the house is nonsense. You want to let the women take care of this? Let me tell you, that's not the way it is. If you want to work it, you have to work as a team. If you don't do that, you don't have anything. You've got to put the work in to get the results out. That means from both parents. And it's not 50 percent each, it's 100 percent each. You've got to put the work out. When you do, then you're going to see the results. If you sit home and let your spouse do the work, you won't see anything but a bunch of sorrow. That's the way I feel about it and I think that's the way that Catherine feels about it.

Catherine: By working together, we've seen dramatic changes in Earl, even though he wasn't actively going to a 12-step program. He saw our behavior changing. I'm sure he was pleased by it. He even started putting out more effort, too. If he's not working at a paying job, then he works around the house. We have to remind him, but we don't get that much resistance either.

Vern: When Catherine and I got out of Earl's face, stopped domineering, and allowed him to either succeed or fail on his own, then he began to display a better attitude and better communication skills. His failure at school to get passing grades, if and when he ever attended, changed to where this last semester he made honor roll. It was because he was able to focus. He wasn't having the confrontations at home with his parents, and was able to commit to the fact that he needed to succeed. He chose, on his own, to do that with school work. Earl has made great progress, and that progress is a direct result of our staying out of his way and allowing him to grow.

Letting Go

A Widow and Her Sons

I have four children, all boys. Until I came into recovery in 1977 from my own alcoholism, I thought I was a first-rate mother. What preys on my mind now is that practically all of the alcoholic women I know are very aware of the damage they may have created in their families, and especially with their children, by their own alcoholism.

In our family, there was a lot of drunk, loud fighting between my husband and me. I read somewhere that that's extremely bad for the kids. There was also some physical abuse. I've been hit more than once, always when both of us were drunk. These are the memories that the kids have.

By the time I became consciously aware of the fact that alcohol was a problem for all four of my sons, I was three years sober myself. I should have seen it earlier. My husband died four years later. We never discussed the fact that any of our sons were alcoholics or addicts.

I remember one episode particularly. When my second son, Ian, had his sixteenth birthday we had a little party with a specially decorated cake. I didn't understand that Ian was drunk when he came in, but he was absolutely in a rage about something. I still have a memory of his smashing his hand in that cake. I don't know what he was mad about, maybe the fact that we were making a fuss over his sixteenth birthday. It's not too unusual for a boy that age to be emotional anyway. Maybe he was feeling, "God damn, you never did anything for me before." I didn't recognize then that he was an alcoholic. As time went on, I began to see other things that were happening with my children.

Kurt

The biggest example is my third son, Kurt, who is now in recovery. Born in 1958, he's been jailed innumerable times. When not incarcerated, he lived in a neighboring ghetto for awhile. During the hippie period, he was in a kind of commune. Another time he was one of those homeless people living on the edge of town. There used to be a lot of them down there. They'd come up during the day and hang out in a little park in the center of town. It really hurt to drive by and see him. I couldn't do anything about it. Watching your kids drink, you wonder when, or if, it's ever going to stop. It's just a hideous thing to go through.

Kurt was actively into heroin for a period of three or four years. To make money for heroin, he would deliver it. People would tip him with money, or heroin, to go into the ghetto and get heroin for them.

At times Kurt has lived with me when he's been down and out. On two or three occasions he was drunk, which really scared me. Then he would move on and go somewhere else or get in jail. Occasionally I'd give him very small amounts of money for food, knowing at least part would go for alcohol and drugs.

What I had visualized and been afraid might happen, is that he'd be passed out drunk in the gutter somewhere and a car would run over him. So for years I maintained his Blue Cross premiums to pay for hospitalization insurance. It dated from way back so the premiums weren't high. About three or four years ago, he was very drunk and as he was crossing a major commercial avenue, he was hit by a car. The driver, an older man, didn't see him.

Kurt's forehead hit the windshield. He had a big blow to the head. Of course the ambulance came immediately and they took him to the hospital. He was there for a couple of months. He wasn't in his right mind for something like forty days before he came around and realized where he was. It was quite frightening. But that was what I had carried the Blue Cross premiums for.

He also had a broken leg which healed eventually. I thought, "Oh God, this will really wake him up." I kept him at home with me while he was recovering. He didn't drink and I felt, "This is great."

But there was one unfortunate incident. While Kurt was staying with me, he stole about $300 by writing checks from my checkbook and forging my name. I tend to believe it was his girlfriend who put him up to it. The bank wanted to call the police, but I refused even though I was furious with Kurt.

After he recuperated, Kurt drifted off and began drinking again. That phase went on for less than a year. I don't know what finally happened to turn him around. Something got to him. It's that realization that you're an alcoholic and this is the situation you're in. You never realize how bad things are when you're going through it.

These days Kurt works as a receiving clerk for a charitable organization that collects used goods from people cleaning out their closets and attics. It's strictly a minimum-wage job. This week Kurt is celebrating his third year of sobriety. I think he's got the big picture at last. He lives in a nearby trailer park. He's not good about going to AA meetings regularly, but I let him know. I see him all the time. He comes over and helps me with little things. He sort of sustains me.

Bradley

The oldest boy, Bradley, was born in 1955. Bradley is a family name. I don't really have a close relationship with him. He has much more control over his drinking, but I think there are times when he drinks to excess. Bradley's a geologist like his father, and is the only one of my sons who finished college. It's a disappointment to me that the other three never finished college. Currently Bradley is trying to establish a consulting firm. I can't imagine that he would let drinking get in the way of his career.

He and the woman he lived with for four or five years, and by whom he has one child, were never legally married. To a great extent that's been his choice. Bradley and the woman broke up, and she recently moved out of state. There was just too much tension, and it was very hard on their daughter. It's better that they're not living together. Their daughter will be six soon. She lives with her mother. I saw them recently, and the little girl seems much calmer.

Ian

My second son, Ian, who was drunk at his sixteenth birthday party, was born in 1957. He now lives up in the northern part of my state. He's the only son who's legally married. He and his wife have two children.

Ian is an alcoholic; he knows that. He's simply awful when he gets drunk—just like I was. He drinks far too much and gets really disgusting and outlandish when he's drunk. I just hate it.

I've invited him to go to meetings of AA. He's not quite ready, but he seems receptive to the idea of AA. He hears me talk about it and I can see that he understands what I'm saying. He gets the idea. I can imagine the day when he too will join AA. I think it would be great if he could, because he's very unhappy the way he is. Ian's wife has told me that she was wild in high school, but today doesn't drink anything.

How does Ian support himself? At one period of time there was considerable building and exploration geology going on in this area, though there's not as much activity now. Somehow Ian came by a very small-bore drilling rig. Partly through people he knew through his father and so on, he connected with a bunch of geologic exploration outfits who were quite active at the time. He made a lot of money drilling, and saved it.

This enabled him and his wife to put money down on a small piece of property they have up north. I call it a ranchette. It's a little place, fifteen acres, off by itself—a really lovely place out in the country.

Now that the drilling business has dried up, Ian's options are being reduced. He has no real skills. However, his wife knew how to start a gardening business, so they moved to the ranchette. Ian didn't want to stay around here, anyway. He hated the noise and the traffic. The gardening business does OK, but I hope that if Ian ever gets sober, he can do better.

David

David, the youngest, was born in 1960. He's been with Kay about nine years, but they're not married. She says the idea of marriage terrifies her because of a bitter divorce between her parents when she was growing up. Kay is enormously interesting, talented, and bright. She has a Ph.D. That impresses me. I'm very fond of her. She loves to party and have a good time. She loves David. Kay takes good care of my boy.

Through drinking buddies, David met a man who owns lots of houses and apartments around the city. David does everything for him: carpentry, plumbing, installing carpets, painting, and so on. At one time Kay and David lived in one of the apartments. Then they saved enough to buy a very nice house.

David is full of denial about his alcoholism. When David gets drunk, he'll start haranguing. He gets up on a soapbox. We used to phone each other once a week, but then he says the same thing over and over. Kay drinks, too. She'll get drunk at parties, but whether that means anything or not, I don't know. She also uses marijuana. Her father, whom she sees only rarely, lives in a charming little fishing port way up on the north coast. Kay loves to go there, and to smoke marijuana with her father. That horrifies me, the idea of a child smoking marijuana with her parent. But they love to get together and do marijuana.

Relationships

As far as relationships between my sons, it's unfortunate. Kurt is something of a scapegoat for his brothers. They call him a street bum and so on, which he was. Now they don't know what to make of his sobriety, so they snarl at each other. I wish it were one big happy family, but they're four boys. At least David and Ian enjoy getting together. They share a love for fishing, but the whole point is, they get together and drink.

One thing I think all of my kids got from both Frank and me is prudence about money. I can complain about the drinking but at least they're extremely good about money.

For a long time I'd react to my sons' alcoholism by lecturing them a lot about AA and recovery. It's only very recently that I've shed that sanctimonious, judgmental attitude—since I got sober.

Detachment with Love

A Father Regains His Life

I'm a parent of an alcoholic. I'm also the brother of an alcoholic, the son of an alcoholic, and the grandson of an alcoholic. I've been the husband of an alcoholic. So I have good roots in addictive disease.

Before I got to Al-Anon, I looked at my son George's problem as being "boys will be boys." When I was a teenager, I'd done crazy things, too. I didn't think George was doing anything wrong or dangerous, so I was entirely lenient.

I remember one night he was necking with his girlfriend in the back of a movie theater. The girlfriend's aunt came along and separated the two and took the young lady out of the theater in the middle of the movie in the middle of whatever they were doing. George went immediately to a pizza parlor and, I guess, was looking like he'd had a rough day. A few people bought him a pitcher of beer, and another pitcher after that. When he was driving home, he picked up a couple of none-too-healthy companions from his high school. A police car began to chase them and the companions convinced George that he could lose them. A total of six police cars were eventually involved. George was finally caught when the cops put a police car on the diagonal in the middle of the road. That brought him to a screeching halt.

Later, he told me that he was going to stop; the police didn't have to do that. I didn't take the whole thing seriously, which was not an appropriate reaction.

I started in Al-Anon because of my wife, Mary, who had entered an alcohol treatment program. I knew Mary had a lot of problems, but I had believed that when she got her act together everything would be all right. Discovering my wife was an alcoholic was a big deflator for me. I had a new feeling of insecurity.

At first I thought Al-Anon was taking roll and that if I didn't attend, the hospital would have something to say about my wife's treatment, so I went. Even though I wasn't an alcoholic and am not an alcoholic now, I also attended AA meetings, because I wanted to be a part of my wife's recovery.

I came into Al-Anon as a "Winnebago Man." A Winnebago man is totally self-contained. He doesn't need anybody to help him. I was pretty grandiose in how I thought of myself and how well I could handle the world. For about three weeks, I maintained this "I don't need you to help me" attitude. I didn't tell anybody what was happening. In fact, since I didn't even know what was going on in my own life, I couldn't quite grasp the need for other individuals.

In 12-step meetings they say, "Be of service to others," "Set up the chairs," "Clean the ashtrays," and "Help make coffee." I began doing those things because I felt it was necessary to be grateful. It was important for me to be humble, because of the grandiose attitude I came in with. I felt useful by helping to set up chairs, put tables together, and have the room ready for a meeting. I think I needed to find some way of deflating myself.

Eventually, I found a sponsor. In the beginning, I thought of him simply as a friend who was willing to listen to me talk. It was the first time I ever talked with anyone about my brother's and father's alcoholism. He was my tutor. My self-esteem had been totally shattered. It was a painful experience to find out I was married to an alcoholic, more than I could handle with my inability to talk to anybody.

In about four months, I erroneously considered myself well enough versed in Al-Anon to give it up. It didn't take long for me to realize that I needed the meetings, and I went back. I needed to work on myself and to be part of a support organization.

When Mary had about six months of sobriety in AA, George started going to both NA (Narcotics Anonymous) and AA. He was seventeen years old. I have two sons and two daughters, but George is the only one with addictive disease.

For me, discovering that George was an alcoholic/addict was like being hit by a truck. I could hardly handle the fact that my wife was an alcoholic, much less my son, too. I took on all the guilt for George's activities. I felt that I should have done things differently, that I was responsible. It was a scary time for me. If I hadn't had Al-Anon, I don't think I would have survived. I felt overly responsible for everything that was happening.

George would get a few clean and sober days together, and then he would slip. Through Al-Anon, I finally got the sense that I had to let go. This was easier for me than it was for my wife. I told George he'd have to leave; he would have to get clean and sober before he was going to be welcome around the house. My wife could not agree. Many times she moved him into the garage without my knowledge, and then would have to order him out again when he got loaded and obnoxious.

George eventually joined the Army and found some new chemical delights. He was a corpsman so he had access to drugs, absolutely free and provided by Uncle Sam. He took advantage of that. Some of what he used was tremendously dangerous stuff and could have cost him his life. He was taking a lot of risks.

After he left the army, he continued to get into trouble. He was entitled to go to the Veterans Affairs hospital for treatment, and one time when he was getting loud and obnoxious in public I decided to take him there. As the medical officer did the intake, George was taking his boots off; then all of a sudden, out of nowhere, he threw his boots at the doctor. The medical officer pressed a button and four guys who looked like middle-aged football players arrived to quiet him down. I realized then that I just couldn't handle him anymore.

Another time, George was very belligerent and was trying to beat up my youngest son, who was probably about forty pounds lighter. George had thrown a five-foot wide bench through the front window. Then he had my second son on the ground and was trying to strangle him. That night we all agreed to press charges and to make George responsible for those actions.

The six months of jail time he received turned out to be the first and only time he'd ever arrived at being anything close to six months clean and sober. He didn't want to use in jail, because he was afraid of being caught and getting a longer sentence.

One night, after George got out of jail, he called me crying. He asked me to pick up his things at a local hotel. I knew something serious had happened. The woman who managed the hotel told me she didn't like having to evict him, but he had spent the whole week not leaving his room and not using the toilets, which were down the hall. He'd also been disturbing people all night long for a week. There was a kindness and a softness about her that registered with me. I picked up George's sea bag. That night I didn't think I would have a son by the end of the week.

I decided I had to get to an Al-Anon meeting. I was early and sat down in a chair. The guy sitting next to me said, "If you sit there, you're going to have to chair the meeting." (To chair means to tell all or part of your story.) The timing was perfect. I just poured myself out. I sensed there were people there who understood where I was coming from. I felt my Higher Power had helped me at just the right point.

Later, George moved up to the state of Washington. He was drinking occasionally, but he was in an AA group where there were people who really understood him. Regardless of what he was like or what he was doing, the AA group was there for him. He finally got to the point where he had five years clean and sober.

Another time, George woke me up at six o'clock in the morning to tell me that he was going to commit suicide. He was in Washington, and I was in California. From the way he talked, I believed this was something that could happen. He had never made a statement like that before. A little further in the conversation, he said that someone from AA was knocking on his door. When I heard that, I decided that I did not have to worry; I knew he would be all right and that I needed to take care of myself. I tried to reach my sponsor, but he wasn't available. I finally ended up in an Al-Anon meeting, spilling out my pain. I had a lot of it. After I talked, I still didn't feel better. Then a young woman, with kids about four years old, shared about living with an active alcoholic for seven years. Somehow or other, she took all my pain away. I realized that I was not the only person living with this problem. It was a powerful experience. I haven't seen that woman for years, but I always carry her number in my phone book. I haven't called her, but I guess it's a security thing I need. I'm very grateful for that.

When George had about two-and-a-half years clean and sober, his wife died from diabetes. I felt it was a blessing that they had no children for George to deal with. I worried about whether he could get through the situation without drinking or using, which he did for another two-and-a-half years. Then for the next five years he lost his sobriety. It was a shock for me. He'd been clean and sober so long that I took it for granted he would probably continue to be.

At first, he stopped going to AA. Over the next couple of years, he'd be sober for a few weeks and then relapse. Earlier this year he turned around. As it happened, two or three people from his original home AA meeting had moved into his area, and they got on his case. What a miracle! You almost think something isn't going to happen and suddenly people are placed in your life who are exactly what you need. Over the years, George couldn't have made it all alone. I know I couldn't.

George has other problems besides addictive disease. When he was five years old, he was hit by a pickup truck, which injured his jaw and one side of his head. He was in a coma for about three weeks. We were told that much of his capacity to make judgments was impaired, and yet in sobriety he makes decisions that he's not supposed to be able to make. He still has psych problems, but he's on medication which helps him. When he mixes the medicine with alcohol, he can become violent. He's been that way a couple of times with his new wife. When this has happened, he has suffered some consequences that have caused him to back off of solving problems that way.

He continues to use the VA hospital. He thinks quite highly of the people there. They have provided a lot of help for him over the years.

Today, George and I keep in touch mostly by phone. Long ago, I stopped preaching and lecturing. I know I am not able to control his actions. Sometimes we talk two or three times a week, and then several weeks go by before we talk again. It varies. I have gone to visit him a few times.

Eighteen years ago, I would never have dreamed that I would be working as an alcohol and drug counselor in a residential transition house, mostly for young people. I remain active in Al-Anon, whose fellowship gave me back my life. I will always be grateful.

Learning to Care
for Oneself

A Mother Saves Herself

My name is Mai. I am an Asian woman married to a caucasian American for twenty-five years. He is a successful professional engineer. He travels a lot, so I'm often the only parent around for our children. We have two sons—Tom, who is twenty-two, and Don, almost eighteen. Both of our sons are alcoholics and addicts, but my husband is in denial about this. I met my husband in China. My father was a violent, abusive alcoholic who terrified me, but I never told my husband about this.

Until eight years ago I knew only how to take care of other people, especially my husband and my children, but also my mother, my sisters and brothers, my boss, the people I work with, and so on. That's what Asian women do. I wanted to be a perfect wife and mother. I wanted to do everything so my husband and sons would love me. I was hungry for love, so hungry I would do anything for everybody.

I was superwoman. My husband and my sons didn't have to do a thing. I waited on them hand and foot. They could come home and sit down and I'd have a beautiful dinner ready. I ironed and cooked and cleaned. If I asked by husband to go out, and he said, "No," I'd just stay home and be sad.

One time I wanted to drink to see how it feels. I tried one drink and I almost died. I hated it. Then eight years ago, my whole life began to change dramatically. My older son, Tom, was then fourteen, and I became aware that he was an alcoholic and drug addict. He would stay out all night. I always waited up for him. I knew exactly what time he came in.

I tried to save my son. Finally, I put him into Juvenile Hall because he was stealing. I found out he was in a gang. There were five gang members, and they were stealing. I recorded a telephone call of them talking about stealing, and I called the police. The judge said to

my, "Why did you do this?" I said, "I work hard. Stealing is wrong."
The judge said he wished all parents were like that.

I was afraid the gang members would try to get me for what I
had done. I told Tom, "If they come after me, they better kill me, because if they just wound me, I'll be after them."

At Juvenile Hall, I was referred to a counselor. She listened to me
and asked, "What do you do for yourself?" I said, "Nothing. I work,
work, work all the time." She told me to start changing some things.

"Lie down and do nothing, first for only five minutes, then ten,
fifteen, and so on until you can do nothing for one hour." She also
asked me to make a list of things I wanted to do just for myself, not
for anybody else. When I did one, I crossed it off the list. She would
call me and ask about my list, how many I had crossed off.

The counselor also told me to go to Al-Anon meetings. She said
I needed Al-Anon to save my life. "You can't save your son," she
said. So eight years ago I went to my first Al-Anon meeting. I just
sat there and cried. That's all I would do. I was very angry. Everybody there was smiling and seemed so happy. They said, "Learn to
let it go," but I couldn't. For a year and a half I sat in the meetings
and cried. Finally, I picked up the message of letting go and started
to apply it to my life. My life really and truly changed and I became
happier.

I began to let go of my son. I set boundaries. I told him to be home
at midnight, and if he wasn't home he could stay outside. It was very
hard for me, but I had to do it. Tom got into deeper trouble. He was
sentenced to a locked facility. I continued to go to Al-Anon and joined
a codependents' group. Also, I went to AA meetings to find out about
the disease of alcoholism. Sometimes I went to meetings five times a
week. I read all the books.

This program has changed my life completely. I learned to let go
of trying to control so many things—my job, my husband, and my
children. I learned that I have no control over others. I can't cure the
alcoholics and addicts in my life and I can't fix them. My sons are still
drinking. They live at home right now, but my life is not wrapped up
in theirs.

I began to learn how to take care of myself. At first, I felt guilty. I
felt selfish. But slowly, I recovered. I do a good job now of taking care
of myself. For the last thirty years, I never knew what life is, but today I am very happy.

I used to work seventy-five hours a week. The reason I worked
such long hours was because I didn't want to deal with my anger and

frustration and worry. Some people eat when they get frustrated; some drink. I couldn't drink. I couldn't eat. So I worked. Work covered my feelings.

Until I slowed down and let go of other people's problems, I didn't know my real feelings. I was a workaholic to avoid my feelings. I didn't trust people. I was insecure so I would protect myself. I wouldn't let people get close to me. I couldn't tell people how I felt. Now I can. Before, if I didn't like something, I would still do it. Now if I don't want to, I say, "I'm not going to do that."

Also, I used to be like this: If you are happy, I am happy. My happiness depended on you. All my emotions depended on others, but not anymore. Today if my sons come home and make me mad, I can say, "I'm very mad at you right now. I need to leave and cool down."

Before when I would get mad, I'd go crazy. I'd punch a hole in the wall. I'd slam the door. I'd scream. Now, I don't have to.

Today I only work twenty hours a week. I have time to sit down and read a book, or just do nothing. I love to crochet. In my free time I go to the movies. Once a month I treat myself and go to a good dinner by myself.

Sometimes there's a family crisis, but I'm mixed up only a couple of days and then I am fine. I may get deeply depressed and return to the same track, but I can recognize it and tell myself, "Stop. Don't get hooked into their lives." That's a drastic change for me. I never dreamed I could be like I am now.

Next month I'm going to Europe again. I tell my husband, "From now on, I'm going to travel around the world as long as I live, to see things." Recovery for me is incredible. My sons are unhappy at the change in me. They say I'm very selfish. My husband is really upset because I used to be a doormat. I don't do that any more. I make sure everybody has chores around the house. I don't wait on my family like I used to. I tell them, "Dinner is right there. If you wish to eat, please serve yourself."

I work on the 12 steps really well and I read the books. I have a special friend in Al-Anon. We go out and talk. My mother-in-law said, "You have changed so much. I don't know what kind of program you go to, but I am so glad you have changed." I'm not hyper like I was. I'm not angry. I carried that anger inside of me for so many years.

The change even applies to my job. I see my boss going around in circles and I think, "I used to be like that." Sometimes I get wrapped up in her problems, but I say to myself, "Stop it! Stop it!" I am able to see myself and stop.

I've worked at the same place for eighteen years. My boss said, "I don't know what you do, but you are so mellow now." It's just letting go of anger. Anger is a killer. It leads to depression and trying to control. Once I wanted to control people's lives, but now I don't.

I can let go the same way with my younger son, Don. He came home one day very drunk. At first, I was screaming and yelling. Then I told myself, "Stop! It's unacceptable for me to act like this," and I let it go. Instead Don and I talked. Before, I couldn't do that.

Recently my husband and I were talking about Tom. My husband said, "Well, if Tom doesn't go to college, you have to push him."

I said, "You know what? I have no control of his life. All I have control of is my life."

And my husband answered, "You can't talk like that. You do too have control."

"No," I said, "he's twenty-two years old." And I just let it go.

Letting go is hard for my husband to understand. He won't go to the program. It's hard for me, too, because I am recovered now. Once we were arguing and fighting and I told him, "I am not like I used to be. You try to push the buttons to make me crazy. I'm not. I have a program to work on now."

"That program makes you sick," he said. "You only learn how to ignore me."

"No," I answered, "it makes me well. It makes you sick but it makes me well."

The changes in me affect my marriage. I used to serve my husband. Now I don't serve him anymore. He's not happy. I know why I used to take care of him and serve him. I just wanted his love. He was happy, but I was not. Today I can see how different I was back then. I thought we might get a divorce because of my changing.

Finally, I told my husband, "I don't try to change you, but my life is different since I found the Al-Anon program. If you're not happy, then you can leave. We'll just split everything up. I'm a hard-working woman. I'm not going to fight. No more." He's never said another word about divorce. When I see now how much I've recovered, and I look at my family and the people around me, I feel for them. I wish they would save their lives. But they have to do it for themselves.

Tom is still drinking. He might use drugs, too. I tell him, "As long as you stay in my house you don't use here. Do it somewhere else. I don't want to see it. If you want to die, go ahead. I have no control of you." He pays rent and that's it. I don't get in his business. I don't pay his bills. I don't do anything.

Don doesn't drink at the moment. But I tell him, "If you drink, you can move out. You are still young."

What I have done with my life in the last eight years is unusual for an Asian woman. It's very special for an Asian woman to go to Al-Anon. When I first came to the program, I never dreamed about taking care of myself. My intention was just to fix my son—to help him recover, to help him want to be well, to help him become a decent person. But in the long run, I was helping myself. Today I even tell Tom, "Thank you for saving my life. If you hadn't gotten in trouble, I would never have found Al-Anon." I would probably still be working eighty hours per week, doing everything for everybody else and nothing for myself.

Last week my older son asked me if I could let him borrow $3,000. I told him, "I love you, but I don't have the money." (I do have the money, but I won't give him the loan.) The reason he needed money was because he owed a lot on credit cards. He said he'd pay me 10 percent.

"Even if you pay me fifty percent," I said, "I don't want it. You have a job. You support yourself. You pay the debt." Without this program I would have said, "Sure," and given him the money right away.

Don has one more year of high school. He's a very good student. Once in a while he goes on a drunk. It's hard to deal with an alcoholic. The behavior is terrible. Now that I'm in Al-Anon, I can see how the drinker's mood changes. I say, "Excuse me, you don't have to be like that in this house, OK?"

Thank God I have Al-Anon. If I didn't have this program, I would probably be dead by now. I was so sick. I have to keep this program for the rest of my life.

Learning on the Job

A Single Father of Five

I was born into a loving nonalcoholic family and saw no real problems with alcohol while I was growing up. We went to church, though we were never forced to, and we usually looked forward to it. I had a good relationship with my Higher Power. My parents did drink but I never saw alcohol abused. They always had a glass of wine before dinner as they went over the events of the day. Now, in their eighties, they still have the same tradition.

I am a middle child with an older brother and a younger sister. We were never allowed to drink until we were of age. Neither my brother nor my sister has a problem with alcohol; but ironically each of us has one child with an alcohol or drug addiction. My siblings' spouses have no drinking problem, but I feel I married a full-blown alcoholic. During college I did my share of drinking but failed to acquire a taste for beer, so a lot of the time I stuck to soft drinks. I had no interest in bars and wasn't inside one until I was twenty-six. I had a good social life just the same.

By the time I reached thirty, I was about the last singles holdout in my group and decided it was time to think about marriage. That Christmas I finally asked my future wife out. We had a very merry Christmas with a whirlwind romance. Years later I realized Jean's drinking was excessive from day one. Married life was very different for me. Jean was a chronic bar drinker. In an effort to keep her out of bars, I went for broke and we bought her dream home. That helped for awhile because Jean wanted everyone to come see her new "palace." We did a lot of entertaining. When most people were buying milk in gallons we were buying liquor in gallons. Thinking back, it's amazing to me how fast my wife could seek out the serious drinkers. My anger toward all of this did not appear until years later.

I next decided the best thing to stop her drinking was a child. The pregnancy did suspend the drinking, but only because she had gestation diabetes and a good Mormon doctor who put the fear of God in her. I would guess that within twenty-four hours of Bobby's birth,

110

Jean resumed drinking. Motherhood never really set in for Jean. She had absolutely no interest in nursing the baby or staying home. I tried to be supportive and encouraged her to take a night or two off with her friends while I took care of the baby. This seemed to work pretty well until she forgot to come home a time or two. She would also leave Bobby alone during the day. It was soon apparent she had found another man.

Our divorce was the hardest time of my life. I wish I had known about Al-Anon then, but I seriously doubt that I would have gone. I finally decided that I owed it to my son to sue for his custody. It wasn't too hard to prove his mother had a drinking problem. By the time the divorce was over, Jean and her next husband had left town.

The next four years were among the happiest I've known. I ran into an old friend from college who was a recent widow. Nancy didn't drink and was very loving to my son. We married and soon had a family of our own—a girl and three more boys. Bobby's mother was almost nonexistent. He saw her three or four times a year. Then, right after the birth of our fourth child (my fifth), my second wife died tragically, leaving me with five children under the age of seven. The baby was only five weeks old. Thus began my life as a single father.

After much thought I moved my family to a new location. I obviously needed help with the children, and ended up using housekeepers from an agency. Immediately after hearing of my wife's death, Jean suddenly was hell bent on coming back. I'd had enough counseling to know that if she returned, it would be only until something better came along. Six months later I realized that things weren't working out with housekeepers, so we moved once again, this time to be near my mother. I bought a home and had it completely remodeled before we moved in. This is really the only home my children remember.

We were now closer to my ex-wife, however. I had to lay down the law that she was not welcome at my home. She could meet Bobby at my mom's house. I also specified what hours she could call and made it very clear she was to talk only to Bobby, and not upset my other children. We had several arguments because she felt she had the right to call and talk to her child any hour of the day or night. About this time, Bobby began having troubles in school. I immediately started counseling and even tried to include Jean, but the sessions were terrible because she wanted to talk mainly about our divorce which was then eight years in the past.

During Bobby's last year in grammar school, we attempted to include his mother again, but all she wanted to do was argue. By the time Bobby entered junior high school, he was going to see his mom almost every other weekend and she was calling very often. Unfortunately, most of her calls were intended to undermine me. The beginning of high school was disastrous for Bobby. Matters grew steadily worse. Several times the school left a message to report absences.

Bobby joined a church group, which I felt would benefit him; but he was coming home later and later, stating they were going out to coffee. I finally said 10 P.M. on a school night was late enough. Things just got worse and soon Bobby was returning at 1 and 2 A.M. from "coffee." It was obvious the "coffee" was having a bad effect on him. I called one of the church leaders and discovered Bobby hadn't been there for weeks. Later I learned there was a group using church as an excuse to get out and then the kids took off. Bobby claimed he had reformed and wanted to return to the church group so I dropped him off and saw him go in the door. A few minutes later he was gone again.

Bobby dropped out of the church group because it was obvious both drinking and drugs went on there and the church refused to do anything about it. Four years later, that church still has a reputation for allowing the drinking and drugging kids to meet there even though the church staff has no training in helping them.

Bobby desperately wanted to have a New Year's Eve party. I sat down with him and his friends and set the rules. The party would be in our garage. Guests were to enter through the house. I made it quite clear there was to be no drinking and no smoking. Anyone who left was not to return. I was to have a list ahead of time of everyone attending. I spent a fortune on that party and even bought non-alcoholic champagne. The kids did a beautiful job of decorating but I became a little suspicious because it seemed some of the older ones were calling the shots. Several parents phoned beforehand, and I went over my rules and took their numbers.

The party started out well, but I became concerned when some of the kids came in the house to use the phone to check with their parents and were exaggerating how well-behaved they were. Then the kids all decided they needed some better music and took off. While they were gone, I checked out the garage and found cigarette butts everywhere. I was extremely upset. When the kids returned, it was obvious Bobby had been drinking. Suddenly, the party was awfully quiet. I went out to the garage. The kids had all jumped the fence and left.

I started calling the parents I had numbers for. One was a policeman. It later came out that the grandmother of the group's ring leader had told several parents that she was coming over to check on the party. I never saw the woman. Most of the kids showed up at about 2 A.M. and the grandma who was supposedly checking on everything came home roaring drunk. We had several incidents where this grandmother was supplying the kids with booze. I finally sent her a certified letter, saying in no uncertain terms that my kids were not to be at her house and her kids were not welcome at mine.

During this time, my son's grades were going down the tubes and I was getting no support from the school. One administrator told me in front of Bobby there was nothing wrong with a kid cutting once in a while. I did get Bobby into some heavy-duty counseling and that helped. At the same time my ex-wife was calling at 2:00 or 3:00 in the morning, extremely drunk, demanding to talk to her son. She also phoned the school continually, telling them what a jerk I was.

At Easter that year, I took my five children on a cruise. Before we left, Bobby was complaining to the counselor. She looked at him and said, "I'm forty-eight years old and have never been anywhere. If you don't want to go, you can stay with my husband and I will go with your dad." Bobby quickly changed his tune. I felt that counselor was worth every dime. The cruise was a turning point for me. I remember the last night on the ship, just thinking of jumping overboard because I simply could not control my son. He was bringing the whole family down.

Bobby finally asked to live with his mom. We discussed this with a counselor who helped us set some guidelines. The school year ended with Bobby's mother arriving in the middle of the night and taking him. I refused to contribute to Bobby's support because I had already supported him half his life without any help from Jean, and I felt the money would only go to support her habits. Jean balked at this, saying I was unreasonable. A few years later, my decision is exactly what the courts dictated.

About a month before Jean took Bobby, I decided to attend an Al-Anon meeting. A friend at work had encouraged me. I was hoping to learn how to deal with my ex-wife. I'd tried a couple of open AA meetings. They didn't seem to help at the time, but years later they still stand out in my mind. One of the first things I heard at Al-Anon is that you don't have to answer the phone when you know a drunk is calling. I quietly had another phone line installed, put an answering machine on the line my ex used, and then turned the bell off when we went to bed. That was the best money I ever spent. I don't think Jean ever realized what I'd done.

I really enjoyed a meeting where issues of ex-wives and kids came up often. I didn't feel so alone. Somewhere along the line I learned I needed to set some boundaries with all my kids and with my own mother. After school was out my mother-in-law took the four younger children to Hawaii for a month. Bobby was with his mother. It was the first time I had been home alone in a long time. I decided just maybe I could do ninety Al-Anon meetings in ninety days. At this same time, there was a court hearing regarding Bobby. The petition Jean had filed was full of lies. I was very upset but my Al-Anon friends calmed me down. I went into court feeling it was all in God's hands. The judge threw everything out and said we were to go to mediation or else.

The mediator was terrific. I was told that both Bobby and his mother had to see for themselves that the grass is not greener on the other side. Jean was adamant, however, that I would never see our son again and that I was going to pay dearly. The mediator was equally adamant that I was going to see my son or she was going to jail. He had to repeat that about ten times. It was finally decided that Bobby would live with his mom during the school year and visit weekends and vacations.

In searching for different Al-Anon meetings to attend in my ninety days, someone suggested I go to one called Parents Letting Go. I tried to explain my problem was with my ex-wife, but two ladies encouraged me to try it, anyway. They said this particular meeting did them a world of good. My first Parents Letting Go meeting was at a retirement home. I thought all the parents at the meeting lived there, but actually none of them did. Most of them, however, were older than I and all of their kids were older. I bonded with the group and I certainly didn't want to end up with a kid the age theirs were, with the same problems.

I heard a lot of good things at those meetings. At one of the first meetings, a mother talked about her fear that her child would die from his addiction. Another talked about putting her home up as bail for her daughter. Then her daughter disappeared and the mother almost lost her home. I also noticed that those who set boundaries seemed to be happiest even if their kids weren't in recovery.

I work full-time, but I was successful in making my ninety meetings in ninety days. I feel if I can do it, anyone can. I found it was okay not to like a meeting and to seek new meetings. Right after I finished my ninety meetings, I went to a combined AA and Al-Anon conference. This really cemented my relationship with AA and Al-Anon.

Although I had taken several parenting classes, I found that what I learned in Parents Letting Go helped my family a great deal more. I finally learned to say no and make my kids responsible for what they did. I also found that I had been trying to buy off my kids, and I decided I didn't want to do that anymore.

By the time Bobby came for his first visit, I was ready. I sat him down and explained that I loved him but I refused to live the way we had in the past. I set limits. Although it killed me, I told him that if he didn't want to abide by those rules I didn't want him in my home. I explained that his mom made the rules in her home and I made the rules in my home. I was clear that no substance abuse was allowed in my home and that certain people were not allowed.

Jean was furious. In an attempt to make me angry, she gave Bobby his own phone (something I had refused to do). That actually turned out to be a Godsend because I could call him and not be hassled by her. I can't believe how many good conversations we had. I was bound and determined to be a part of Bobby's life even though he lived several hours away. I called the school for an appointment to see his counselor, and was surprised by a very cold reception. I was afraid they wouldn't see me. When I finally met the counselor, it was apparent he was expecting a monster. Once he got over the shock, he was willing to work with me. I sat down and told him the truth. He encouraged me to call at anytime and he wasn't afraid to make long-distance calls to talk to me. It was nice to hear someone say my son had some redeeming features. The school sought and got my permission to put Bobby in a school-controlled class on substance abuse. He did exceedingly well and I believe gave up all abuse for several years.

The hardest thing I had to face was that Bobby had a problem with drugs and alcohol. I became very open about it. I remember talking to the parents of one of his friends and admitting the family secret. Afterwards I feared Bobby would be angry with me because his friend's parents would probably restrict him. As it turns out, I've become very close to these parents. They respect me for my honesty.

I myself changed a lot. I found out yelling didn't accomplish anything, especially when someone was under the influence. Soon after Bobby got into recovery we were able to talk openly, and I feel we both began to express ourselves. He gave me some good pointers with his sister and brothers. We finally agreed not to bring his mother into conversations. Eventually, Bobby acknowledged she was severely addicted to both alcohol and drugs, and he saw the problems her disease caused.

I have now been in Al-Anon four years. Bobby recently turned eighteen. He graduated from high school with good grades. Sadly, his mom didn't live to see this happen. She died of her disease last year at the age of forty-five. Bobby has had some slips since his mom died, but he is aware of the problem and is honest about his slips. His behavior is 1000% better and I think he feels my behavior is 1000% better. I can't blame the disease for everything. After all, he is a teenager. He has definitely talked openly to his siblings and I don't see the problem recurring.

My daughter, Kit, is fifteen. She seems to be very knowledgeable about the 12 steps. She goes quite often to an Alateen meeting a few blocks from our house. Kit's the "mother" of the family and way beyond her years. Kevin, fourteen, is very shy. He's taken heat over Bobby's shenanigans, and would prefer to forget all that has happened. Miles, twelve, is my most outgoing child, and probably has the most potential to be a problem. He's already six feet, three inches tall, and says he can live without that "crap." Rich, the baby of the family, is now eleven years old. Everyone predicted he would have the most troubles because he was only a tiny infant when his mother died. I think he's my best-adjusted kid, though, and has done the best. I think his grandmothers went out of their way to see he got some extra mothering.

I myself am much happier. Most of the time I use in my personal life what I have learned in the Al-Anon program. I still hear something useful at every meeting. Though I don't go to as many meetings as I used to, I read Al-Anon literature and I journal daily. My journal brings me a great deal of happiness when I go back a few years and see how far Bobby and I have come. The kids and I talk very frankly about drugs and alcohol. I think Bobby openly discourages his sister and brothers from using or experimenting. I am convinced my son will get back into permanent recovery but I will accept whatever he does with love. I feel the program has improved the life of our entire family and I will be eternally grateful.

Losing a Son

A Stepmother's Story

The first part of my story is about my stepson Jim. He had such an impact on the rest of our family, that I need to tell about him first. The other members of our family are my husband Steve, my son Kyle, and of course, myself.

Jim

My boyfriend Steve (now my husband) and I were back East when we first met. His son Jim was eleven years old and my son Kyle was five. Steve drank too much and I smoked a lot of pot, so we didn't really question certain things that happened.

After we had been together for about a year, Steve and I moved back to the West Coast with Kyle, leaving Jim with his mother. Then Jim's mother said she was having problems with him. He was drinking and maybe smoking some pot. She couldn't handle him anymore, so she said Jim could come and live with us.

We agreed. Jim thought it would be cool to live with a stepmother who smoked pot. Steve had been a really strict father and disciplinarian in his first marriage. This was his second start and a chance to be different, with a younger woman. However, he continued with his drinking. Neither of us had the judgment that other parents might have had.

We didn't give Jim any firm rules or guidelines, so he started getting into trouble. When he was about thirteen or fourteen, he took my car out when we were not home. He wasn't licensed and he had been drinking. He knocked over a phone pole down the street.

The police came and ticketed Jim for reckless driving and joyriding. They call it "joyriding" when you steal a car from your parents. We had quite a bill from the phone company. I remember I got angry at the time because we were billed not only for the work but also for the phone pole. I told them I wanted the pole, since we had to pay for it. We didn't get it, though. Jim got some kind of fine.

117

Three years or so after moving to California, Steve and I were married. Jim was fifteen and Kyle was nine.

Jim continued to have mild skirmishes with the law, visits to Juvenile Hall, and so on. There was a lot of fighting and a lot of problems. It wasn't so much Jim as the combination of his using and drinking, and parents that weren't in control. Jim's father and I began to fight with each other. There was a constant state of tension in the family. When Jim and I would fight, Steve would feel caught in between. I can't remember anything the fights with Jim were particularly about. While this was going on, Jim occasionally went to stay with friends.

Jim would go through a ritual of quitting, throwing away his papers, pipe, or whatever. "I'm gonna get on the straight and narrow," he would say. As someone who had gone through the swearing off, back and forth, I understood that. However, I was not prepared to be a stepmother. Certainly not of a teenager who was an alcoholic-addict. I had a lot thrust on me. I wasn't capable of doing much for myself, let alone Jim and my other son.

When Jim and I got along, nobody got along as well as he and I did. When we didn't get along, nobody got along as bad as he and I did. We had a very strong connection. There was nothing moderate about it. It was much different than his relationship with his father.

Steve believed it was OK to hit your children, but I didn't. When Steve moved in with me, he learned this. The first time Steve went to hit Jim, I punched Steve and he got a bloody nose. Jim was so pleased. He had been hit by his father for years.

My other son, Kyle, was the opposite—a really quiet kid. He ate a lot and played with toys. He was the opposite of any kind of acting-out kid, almost mute while all this stuff was going on around him.

One time when Steve, Kyle, and I had gone out for the evening, Jim decided to have a party, with a keg. When we drove home, kids and cars were parked all up and down our street. There were a lot of drunken teenagers. At the time, Jim had a job that was fairly decent, at a pizza place. That was where he got the keg of beer. His manager really liked him, so when I went to see her and told on him, she was not going to do anything. But Jim did lose his job and had to pay for some things. To be honest, I don't remember if the police were involved that time or if he just lost his job.

Then Jim and a friend got into trouble. I think Jim was living with a young married couple. The couple themselves were about nineteen years old and Jim was around fifteen. The couple lived right by a potato chip place, and Jim and his friend decided to break into a potato-chip truck. We laughed later at the "Frito banditos." The kids took a whole bunch of boxes of potato chips, but no money or stereos or anything. But the police said it was still breaking and entering. It was a big crime in the eyes of the law. That time Jim did have to stay in Juvenile Hall. We would visit him and it was very depressing. He said he was going to clean his act up.

I don't remember how long he was there, maybe a few days to a week. When he got out he moved back in with us and got a girlfriend who was straight. He started going to school regularly. He had a good relationship with his wood shop teacher. It was good for Jim to have a friend like that teacher because, the truth is, we were not good parents for Jim. We weren't positive role models. We were glad he had that teacher, and a girlfriend who came from a good home.

I remember when Jim was only twelve I found that a girl had spent the night in his bed. Her parents knew she was doing it, and she was only twelve or thirteen! Even in our state of mind as hip parents, that seemed strange. This new girlfriend, Lisa, was really straight and very sweet. She and Jim began going steady. Jim was doing well at school.

He was on a kind of probation, where school was keeping track of him, and so were we. He did something—I don't remember what it was—and I called his probation officer and turned him in. It didn't seem like a very nice thing for a mother to do, but I was just fed up with him. He would move in with the couple I mentioned, then move back home, and so on.

Sometimes Jim would be very, very good with his clean-cut girlfriend and his wood working and his school. Other times he was not so good. One day I had an idea that he was cutting school. It was just one of those intuitive mother flashes. I called the school and he had cut. He almost did it successfully, because he knew a girl in the office who called him in sick. I reported him to the school. I wanted to get him in line.

Another time, when he was in Juvenile Hall, Steve and I went to a Tough Love meeting (see appendix). We thought we could go to one meeting and know it all. They took a hard line. They said when your son is in "Juvie," don't visit, don't make it easy for him, don't bring him the books, and so on. They could have said something else, but that's what I remember. By now my husband's and my own alcohol problems had gotten pretty severe, but we had Jim to focus on. He was the classic scapegoat. I didn't visit him, according to what I perceived Tough Love had said, but I did write a couple of letters.

Steve went to the hearing. Jim was by now seventeen years old. The court decided that Jim needed help and that he should go to a treatment place. There was a facility in a county north of here. We were pushing for that. We thought he should be away from everybody, especially his girlfriend and friends with cars, so he would have less chance of running away.

The authorities agreed to place Jim in a group house for teenagers, but in the town right next to where we lived. Steve and I thought it was the wrong decision for Jim to be so close to his friends. I didn't see him there. When you first are in one of these places you don't get to see family or friends. He stayed a couple of weeks, I guess. Then he ran away. It's exactly what I was worried about. This was in June. We had no idea where he was. We suspected his girlfriend and friends knew, but we did not.

His father's birthday and Father's Day come pretty close to each other. I was feeling bad for my husband, not knowing where Jim was. We didn't want to help Jim run from the law. In fact, we wanted to see him turn himself in. As I recall, he had a certain length of time to turn himself back in, but if he stayed beyond that time they would have a warrant out and he could be incarcerated in a locked facility.

I left a couple of messages with his girlfriend. "Lisa, you don't have to tell me where Jim is or anything, but it would be real nice if he could call his father for Father's Day or for his birthday or something, because we are really worried. Maybe you could encourage Jim to turn himself in. If he gets caught, it's going to be lots worse. But mostly I'd just like you to let him know that we love him."

Jim did call his dad on Father's Day and Steve agreed to meet him at a fast-food place. Steve strongly encouraged Jim to turn himself in. He pleaded, "Turn yourself in. We'll support you. Staying on the run isn't going to help. Please turn yourself in." Jim said, "I really need some money. Could I come work with you today? I'll help you, carry stuff, do anything." Steve replied, "No. I don't want to help you. You are escaped from the place the court sent you. I can't."

Later that same day Jim and his girlfriend and two friends went horseback riding. They were near a lake and decided to go for a swim. I think they had a six-pack of beer or malt liquor. I don't know who drank what or if they smoked pot or did other drugs.

When Jim went into the water, for some reason he left on his long pants, his socks, and his underwear. I guess it was modesty. In my day we would have stripped to our underwear or gone naked. Why anyone would try to swim in long bell-bottoms we don't know.

While he and his friend were swimming out to the middle of the lake, Jim started going under. One of his friends tried to save him but was getting pulled down so he went back to shore. There was a lot of hysteria. The police came, but it was too late. Jim had drowned.

While all of this was going on we knew nothing about it. That evening, we got a call from Jim's very distraught, hysterical girlfriend. I still don't know if Steve didn't want to hear what she said, or if Lisa couldn't tell him what was the matter. My husband just assumed Jim had a problem in the water, and maybe was in the hospital. The next call was around midnight, from the county morgue asking if we wanted to come and identify Jim and pick up his belongings. So our first notification that Jim had died was from the morgue.

Life After Jim's Death

We had a regular funeral for Jim. Steve's parents came from back East. The mortuary was sad because they had sponsored Jim's Little League team. Their name was on the back of his Little League uniform.

When Jim died, Steve and I were in family therapy and in couples counseling. I was also in a group for prescription polydrug abusers. My husband went to a grief support group for parents who had lost children. He encouraged me to come but I said no. Since I was Jim's stepmother for only five years, I thought my husband had a different kind of grief so I didn't go to the group with him.

The reason most marriages split up after the death of a child is that people usually don't grieve the same way. My husband went to work more than ever. I couldn't work. I couldn't even get off the couch. I didn't want to leave the house. I'd urinate in my bedroom wastebasket rather than leave my room. Steve was out at work all the time. If he was home, he was in the garage working or puttering. At first, I thought Steve wasn't grieving since he went to work every day. And Steve thought I was just getting loaded, so how could I care? Finally I made a decision that however Steve grieved and however he needed to handle Jim's death, it was his choice. My husband's drinking escalated and so did my drug use. It got really bad. We had lost our scapegoat, Jim. Without him to focus on, we started blaming each other.

I ended up going to Al-Anon about my problems of living with a husband who was an alcoholic, and losing a son because he was an alcoholic. Yet I was not facing my own problem, prescription drugs.

After three Al-Anon meetings, I came home and told Steve I did-n't think our marriage was going to work. I said, "I've got enough Al-Anon to know I can't tell you what to do and this is not an ultima-tum, but I have a feeling that if you don't quit drinking, we are not going to be able to keep on going like we are."

Steve went to Alcoholics Anonymous that night and has been clean and sober ever since! I stopped drinking and smoking pot, but continued to abuse prescription drugs for the summer after Jim died. Then I gave up and went to AA, too. So within months of surviving the death of a child, we survived early recovery, which can be pretty traumatic itself.

I think it was grace—grace and grit. We had a lot of tenacity. Somebody would tell us, "Your marriage doesn't have a chance. You guys are fighting all the time and you're newly sober." There's a part of both my husband and me that's very stubborn and pretty much the opposite of what you learn in the 12-step programs, because we're willing to stick it out no matter what, almost in defiance. And then there's another part of us that surrenders to certain things.

We still go to therapy and I still hit walls about Jim's death and about being bad parents. I have some acceptance that we did the best we could at the time and that we didn't know any better. There were times when I was loaded or on pills when I knew I was saying or do-ing mean things to Jim. And, of course, my husband has tremendous guilt because Jim wanted to be with him that day. Steve said no be-cause he couldn't help Jim run from the law. So, of course, my hus-band will always wonder if he could have saved Jim.

It takes a lot of therapy and other help to deal with the death of a child. When I was new in AA, I had a problem with some of the things that were said to me. We were just grief stricken and I don't think we needed someone to tell us, "You know, that's God's will," or "Well look, it got you to AA." For a long time my being in AA was tainted by the fact that many people told me I got there because Jim died. It was very confusing. I knew I wanted to be clean and sober and to be in a 12-step program. I went to Al-Anon and AA all the time. But it felt wrong somehow. My son died, so that was my ticket in there. In hindsight I wish I hadn't listened to certain people. If peo-ple had spoken only from their own experience, strength, and hope after actually losing a child, it would have helped me more.

With the death of a child, I don't think I can achieve the serenity and acceptance that you hear about so much in Al-Anon. My accep-tance has to be around his death rather than the fact that he was an addict. I think acceptance comes in pieces. I can't say everything is fine. It's still not fine with me. Whenever I hear in the Promises, "I will not regret the past nor wish to shut the door on it," there's a part of me that says, "I can't imagine any parent who doesn't regret their child's dying."

It's hard to say what particular thing helps—certainly sitting in meetings and hearing other people talk. I think what actually helps me most is when I hear other people say some of the mean things they did to their own children. I realize now that people who are hurt, hurt other people. I still fall back into old patterns, so sometimes when I hear someone share in a meeting, I realize that I am not an evil or bad person. I was a sick person.

Now when I have sadness because it's Jim's birthday or something, it's pure sadness. It's not guilt, just pure grief. Things are better, not worse. When I had guilt, I tried to make rationalizations in my head. Now what I feel is completely in my heart. That's one of the things the 12-step programs have given me, to have these feelings on a pure level.

Kyle was ten when Jim died. My son is a very sensitive kid and he has it in his head that Steve doesn't like to talk about Jim. So sometimes Kyle and I will be together and he will say, "Did I ever tell you this really funny story of what Jim and I did?" and he'll tell me all these funny things. And I'll say, "Oh, you should tell Steve." And he'll answer, "Oh no, I'd never bring up Jim with Steve." I don't know if he has really good intuition about it, or if he's afraid. I don't even know if he's right or wrong. My son and Steve have a great relationship, but Kyle is very protective of Steve in that way.

Steve and I don't talk about Jim much these days. I don't have any fear about it. Steve has never asked me not to discuss Jim, and he doesn't get upset when I do. What Steve and I have now is a wonderful marriage that includes a very good relationship with Kyle.

Seven years after Jim drowned, when Kyle was about seventeen himself, I learned he was smoking pot and had been for awhile. He sat down and told me all about it. It was Mother's Day. He talked for hours. I was upset and surprised and felt like a fool because I once smoked pot and our other son did, yet I didn't know about Kyle. We just talked about it. I shared my own experience, saying, "I hope you don't have to lose what I did to get into AA or NA or whatever. I hope the light comes on for you a little softer."

When Kyle told me, I didn't have a lot of guilt. I remember saying to my husband, "God, I felt more like a fool. He's been doing it all this time under my nose and I didn't notice." I wasn't mad at him and I wasn't that surprised. Some part of me must have known. I just increased my meetings, whether it be Al-Anon or AA. I went and heard how people cope.

The son who was so quiet became more of the acting-out kid. He smokes pot and we know it. He's not outrageous with it. I'm not saying it's good or bad. We don't condone it the way we did with Jim. For one thing, Kyle is now twenty-three. He lives on his own and supports himself. He can come to our house but we don't allow any drugs or paraphernalia. I don't have acceptance of my son's pot but I know I can't control it. I know I can't do anything about it. He knows how I feel. He knows the rules: not around me, not around my house. I won't lend him money. If he says he needs it for rent, I tell him he might take the money and spend it on pot. Any money I give him might go to buy drugs, and I won't do that.

By now, Steve and I have been in 12-step programs for a long time. Our lives get more sane. We worry about Kyle somewhat, but are not focused on it. But we are prepared in case he does start smoking more or moves on to harder things. It could get to be a problem, but we try not to worry about it now. We don't feel guilty that we did something wrong regarding Kyle. It's not our fault. We actually joke about it sometimes. We have a good detachment from it. I guess we had to learn so much and so hard by having Jim die that dealing with Kyle just seems to be built in for us.

I remember saying things to Jim like, "Get out of my house for ever," or "I hate you." I remember having horrible screaming fights. Those are things that you can't take back. It taught me in my marriage that no matter what happens, never leave the house or go to sleep without the fight or hard words being resolved. Even if we can't make up perfectly, we can at least say, "I hope you know I really love you."

Last night my son called me and I was too tired to talk. I wanted to sleep and he wanted to talk to me about his life plans for the future. I tried to tell him, "Honey. I'm really tired. You get up a lot later than I do." Then I remembered Jim, like my guardian angel, and I thought, "Kate, what if something happened to Kyle tonight? What if something happened to Kyle tomorrow? Is it so important to get ten minutes of extra sleep?" So I just lay back and let him talk. Time with your kid is real precious. Time with anyone you love is real precious.

Addictive Disease
Knows No Boundaries

An Alcoholic Mother
of Alcoholic Sons

I am from Thailand. I have five grown children: two sons and a daughter by my first husband, a Thai; and two sons by my American husband. My two Thai sons and one of my American sons have addictive disease.

I am the second daughter in a large family. My relatives on both my mother's and my father's side all have a problem with alcohol, except for my grandmother and my mother. Addictive disease is not uncommon in Thailand. My father was an alcoholic and he smoked opium. He was also a gambler. I myself became an alcoholic and a compulsive gambler, but I've been clean and sober for the past eleven years.

I'm a dancer. My whole family are professional dancers in Thailand. Every time we performed we would get free food, whiskey, and cigarettes. My family was rich until my father lost everything through his addictions. He was like a king among dancers in Thailand, Laos, and Cambodia.

I married a Thai policeman. We had three children—two sons, Mechai and Teddy and a daughter, Amara. I left my husband because he loved to fool around.

After Mechai was born, I started working again to support him, and my mother helped, too. She took care of Mechai a lot because at night I went dancing and singing in bars. I joined a troupe and performed everywhere with them, including Laos. I met my American husband, Terry, at a four-day event in Thailand. Four or five years later we were married. Terry learned to speak Thai. We moved to the United States with Teddy, but left Mechai and Amara with my mother. Eventually Terry and I had two sons, David and Billy.

Teddy

Teddy is an addict. He had a lot of problems with the police, and was in Juvenile Hall. The judge took Teddy away from Terry and me, and placed him in a foster home. When Teddy was eighteen years old, he pulled a knife on a girl, to get the money to buy pot. He was accused of kidnapping and sent to prison for ten years.

Teddy's been out of prison for five years now. He's married and lives nearby, but is clean and sober only off and on. I asked him about it a couple of days ago. He said, "I don't lie to you. I still use, but not as much."

Mechai

When Terry and I bought our house about fifteen years ago, we brought my firstborn, Mechai, to the United States to live with us. Mechai was in his early twenties. In Thailand he already had a problem with drinking and I think other drugs. He continued to drink heavily. I lost a lot of sleep over him. He would go out and drink everyday and come home and fight with me. Then he'd start a fight with Terry. He'd start a fight with anybody. It was bad because I was still drinking myself, and had a very hot temper.

Mechai was way out of control, though. Every time he drank, he'd have a lot of resentment toward me because I divorced his father, the policeman. Mechai never lived with his father, but he'd say, "You don't love me. You don't love my father." That's the way he would talk when he was drinking. Because I married Terry and moved here and left him in Thailand, he didn't want to come to this country.

Finally, I got in trouble with drunk driving and ended up in a hospital treatment program for alcoholism. That was where I discovered Alcoholics Anonymous and when Terry had to go to Al-Anon on my account. Just as my recovery began, I was sentenced to forty-five days in jail. Teddy was also in prison at that time. My daughter, Amara, was already married, but Mechai, David, and Billy were still at home. I brought my mother from Thailand to take care of Billy, who was pretty young.

David is just like his father, Terry. He is quiet and scholarly, and definitely not an alcoholic. Billy was a handful, though, and Mechai was in the middle of his addictions. Because Mechai had no insurance, I could never send him for treatment. We kicked him out of the house many times. My AA sponsor would say, "Kick him out! Don't try to take care of him." My mother always felt sorry for him, though. She'd give him money. My mother was codependent. It's one reason Mechai couldn't get sober.

After I got deeper into Alcoholics Anonymous, Mechai was in and out of AA himself for a long time. Finally, after a very bad drunk-driving accident, he was sent to a psychiatric prison for one year. I never went to visit him. I'd already told him I wouldn't. When he came out he begged me to give him one more chance. He wanted to get sober this time. The other times, I gave in. This time, I did nothing. I never helped him. He wanted to go to AA with me, but I didn't take him to meetings. I let him walk. Terry let go, too. Today Mechai has been clean and sober for two years. He's a 38-year-old miracle.

Billy

When Billy entered high school, he began running with a bad crowd, smoking pot, and having bouts of depression. I've been hospitalized several times in sobriety for serious depression myself, so Billy has inherited that as well as his alcoholism and my bad temper.

I don't know where he got his alcohol when he was in high school. I suppose people gave it to him. You have a lot of that in school. Also, he would steal my money and buy booze. He stole a lot of my jewelry.

Four times Billy was hospitalized for suicidal depression and for drinking and using. He'd be in an adolescent treatment program for thirty days, get discharged and stay clean and sober for a month, then start the whole cycle over again. While abstinent, he would go to AA meetings, but last only a few weeks because he'd say, "I'm too young." (He wasn't yet eighteen years old.)

After the last hospitalization, however, he's been about ten times better even though he hasn't stopped drinking and using entirely, and even though he doesn't go to AA. Before, he was terrible to live with. Now he is more reasonable. He has a job. It's the Thai custom for adult children to live at home until they marry, so Billy and Mechai are still with Terry and me. (David, my one nonalcoholic son, is married and lives in another part of the state. He has two children.)

I had problems with my own recovery, but going to a lot of AA meetings helped. I started in Al-Anon, too, and learned how to stay well. Billy is not my problem anymore. I'm no longer fixing other people's problems. I let God be in charge.

Once I was a Buddhist and used to pray and go to a temple, but when my father died, I stopped. Here in my house I have a Buddha that my father gave me. It's over four hundred years old. I honor this Buddha, but Alcoholics Anonymous is my spiritual life today.

I know now that my relatives in Thailand will probably never get well from alcoholism and drug addiction, and I accept that. Everybody drinks, including two of my sisters and a brother. They want me to come back to visit, but I don't want to even though it's been fifteen years since I saw them. We're different now. I told one sister on the telephone, "I cannot bear to see you die. I love you, but I must leave you alone and you must leave me alone."

Billy may never get completely well, either, and I have also accepted that.

Whose Problem?

A Divorced Mother, An Only Child

I've been a single parent ever since I was divorced from my daughter's father when she was very young. He lived nearby after he remarried, however, and had several more children. Although Jean was our only child, she grew up in close companionship with her half-brothers and sisters. I worked at a major university until I retired several years ago, and have always lived comfortably in an upper-middle-class neighborhood.

Jean's high-school years coincided with the liberal, unrestrained 1960s. Up to then she'd lived a pretty normal life, but during those years she became rebellious and hostile. I tried to be open-minded and tolerant about her rebellion and hostility, followed by the drug scene, strange companions, and stranger behavior. As the years jerked and heaved past, drugs gave way to alcohol and it became harder for me to stay detached. I was trying to guide and protect and shield this child who was no longer a child. I knew, of course, that she had to learn from her experiences, but I thought I could make the learning painless and gentle.

I tried everything I could think of to make my daughter see what she was doing to herself, as well as to me. I tried restricting her drinking with words. "You'll feel bad tomorrow." "You'll damage your liver." "You're losing interest in outside activities." Nothing I did worked. The immediate consequence was increased drinking, which led to my increased desperation to blot out what was going on in order to promote a less tense atmosphere at home. My daughter must have been a lot more stubborn than I realized, since the only response from her was antagonism and hostility.

In addition to alcohol, Jean was heavily into heroin. This frightened and worried me because not only was heroin illegal, but the main source was in a dangerous neighborhood in another town. Street drugs were totally outside my experience.

I had so much guilt over what I felt I had caused my daughter to become. I thought I must have been a bad mother. I couldn't understand why I couldn't control her behavior and why she wasn't able to control her own. I had no real conception of addiction.

I found that I was changing my way of thinking almost unconsciously. I stopped considering this person I lived with as an individual who could think and act independently. Instead, I was trying to communicate with a zombie. I was always frustrated when the rational actions I expected failed to materialize. I continually tried to second-guess what Jean's next move would be and how to forestall it. It was like talking to a person who neither speaks nor understands English. I would automatically start to shout.

When she borrowed money, I made her keep track of it and pay it back. I was shocked when I began to find that money was missing from my purse. There were later shocks as well. But believe me, it is impossible to maintain a permanent state of shock, no matter what the circumstances. I stayed in there, fighting as hard as I could to help her see what she was doing to herself. This went on for longer than I care to remember. It seems that we are both survivors.

Somewhere along the way, I realized that Jean's father had also been addicted to alcohol as well as to prescription drugs. His denial was so strong that he never did ask for help. I was in denial, too. Not knowing anything about alcohol addiction at the time, I didn't recognize his eruptions of temper and erratic behavior for what they were.

Besides the actual addiction, Jean took after her father in violence and unpredictability when she was drinking. More than once she started after me. I learned to keep a suitcase packed so I could escape to a friend's house whenever my daughter went crazy from alcohol. Those last years of her drinking and using were turbulent and scary.

When Jean wasn't drinking or using, she was fairly O.K. She finished high school, then found a job as a nurse's aide. She was a very good worker and liked her job even though in time she started missing shifts. Her supervisor valued her, however, and thus tolerated Jean's absences. Apparently, the hospital didn't realize what the problem was, and I certainly didn't tell them. In fact, her employers didn't have any idea until I had to inquire about Jean's health insurance coverage for inpatient treatment of alcoholism the day my daughter was finally persuaded that she should be admitted to a hospital program.

A few friends and family were aware of what was going on. However, none of them knew any more about addiction than I did. After I found Al-Anon, I came to realize that these well-meaning friends and family members tended to be overly sympathetic about my situation; therefore, they couldn't help me set legitimate boundaries nor offer sound suggestions from their own experience.

After some years of living with my alcoholic daughter, I completely lost hope of being able to do anything for her. I saw myself drowning along with her. Then I found a group of like-minded people in Al-Anon who had the same problem and had managed to survive it. With their help, I learned that one cannot solve another's problems. In time, this led to letting go of my child and unleashing the verbal chains I'd used with her in the effort to restrict her drinking. Watching a person launched on a disastrous course of action is very painful, but I finally knew that if I saved Jean from that course, it would prevent her from learning that it doesn't work.

Something I read helped me realize that "There is no right way to do the wrong thing." Now, when things go wrong, I try to stop and determine whose problem it is. When it's mine, I try to solve it. When it's somebody else's, I try to distance myself from it and refrain from making suggestions.

Jean grew worse and worse. After I'd been in Al-Anon for several years, and with many false starts and slips on the part of both Jean and me, I finally accepted she was either going to have to leave our home and live somewhere else—God knows where—or get treatment. I couldn't go on this way any longer. With the support of friends in AA and Al-Anon, and after tentatively reserving a bed at a hospital-based treatment center, I found the courage to deliver this ultimatum to my daughter.

That morning Jean was still in bed at noon. I think she was so shocked by my decision and firmness that she just caved in. A couple of AA women were there. They stayed with her and drove her to the hospital. She entered a thirty-day inpatient alcohol and drug treatment program. There she gave up heroin cold turkey at the same time as alcohol, and has never gone back to either.

The treatment program was strongly in favor of Alcoholics Anonymous. AA meetings in the hospital and community were mandatory for patients, and Al-Anon, Alateen, and Alatot for families. Sometimes people half-jokingly ask for an Aladog group, since even our pets sometimes seem affected by addictive disease in their masters. In addition to the 12-step groups the hospital offered excellent family therapy groups led by counselors experienced in working with families.

Unlike most family members, I was already very familiar with Al-Anon and understood completely how important and helpful it was. It was always interesting, however, to watch how most family members greatly resisted having to attend support meetings for themselves. "How come? We're not the sick ones!" Then over the weeks, many family members would come to appreciate how skewed and unhappy their own lives had become, and how relief and help were available if they chose to avail themselves of Al-Anon's resources. Patients who were serious about recovery were grateful to see their families willing to do whatever they could to support the healing process for the whole family unit.

Many years ago, while she was still drinking and using, Jean became a follower of a well-known Indian guru or master. She learned how to meditate and she adopted vegetarianism. After the hospital treatment program for addiction, she resumed participation in her meditation group with a clear mind and heart. Through her master she has found a deep and satisfying spiritual path. For the first several years of sobriety, Jean was also active in Alcoholics Anonymous. Now she goes only on special occasions.

Her prerecovery interest and experience in nursing led Jean to complete a rigorous four-year nursing program. She earned her bachelor of science degree, and has been responsibly employed as a nurse in a very large hospital for many years. She hasn't had a drink or fix in the past seventeen years.

Jean and I still live in the same house where there was so much turmoil and chaos. We have our own lives and interests, but we're very good company for each other. We vacation together and have a lot of fun. I'm the homemaker while Jean follows her career.

I've had some health problems and don't get to Al-Anon much anymore, but the principles of the program will never leave me. They saved my sanity.

Too Much Is Enough

Chips Off the Old Block

All three of my children were raised in a home where both parents drank. There wasn't any question as to what priorities we had. Our lives centered around alcohol.

Most of this story is about my youngest son, Steve, and my older son, Thom. My daughter, Christine, is not alcoholic as far as I know, and appears only briefly.

Steve

I remember very clearly an incident when the children were little. One New Year's Eve they were permitted to stay up until midnight and have a small glass of champagne to celebrate. I asked if they wanted a second glass. Steve took a sip of his refill, then stopped and said, "Too much is enough." I think that profound observation described a lot of his later experience—and mine and everyone else's in the family.

One evening, I received a call from the father of one of Steve's playmates, Peter. The boys were ten or eleven years old. Peter's father asked me if Steve had been drinking. I told him not that I knew of. He said that Peter was drunk. I went to my son and said, "Steve, have you been drinking? Peter's father says Peter's drunk." "Well . . . yes," he replied. "Johnny's parents are away and Johnny had a cocktail party. Peter just can't hold his liquor. That's what happened."

At that point, I felt a little bit of pride in Steve. Not knowing that he had been drinking—probably because I was drinking, too—I did not notice any abnormal behavior in him.

My wife and I fell into the trap of thinking we would teach our children to drink responsibly. All through their high school years, we thought it was better that they and their friends drink beer in our home instead of driving under the influence, or looking for someone to buy beer for them.

Friends of my children were always around the house. They were like extended family, and had the run of the place. We had a bar, but it never occurred to us that they would ever drink any of my wine or hard liquor. Maybe they didn't, but they certainly had beer.

While Steve's drinking may not have been recognizable to me, it was to others. I remember getting a call from someone over at the high school one evening. They said he had climbed on top of a phone booth and had obviously been drinking. They asked me to come and pick him up. On the way home I admonished him for "drinking in public."

During Steve's senior year in high school, I ran into the mother of one of his closest friends at a post-season football banquet. She mentioned that she hadn't seen Steve since he was in junior high.

"Good grief," I thought to myself, "I've seen your son. He practically lives over at my house." Of course, the reason was that he was permitted to drink, which was unfortunate.

Shortly after that, I left my marriage and moved to California. I thought Steve was so well-adjusted that he would be all right. He was a good athlete, a good student, and he had a nice girlfriend. I believed that he, of all my kids, would be least affected by the divorce and my moving away. He told his sister that he felt abandoned, and later he confided in me how painful it was to be with his mother, who continued as an active alcoholic for many years.

At the end of his freshman year of college, Steve was in a very serious automobile accident. He was driving, and some of his friends were in the car. The one-car accident was entirely his fault. He was the only one hurt; he suffered considerable facial damage (including the loss of a couple of front teeth) and a fractured skull. He required plastic and prophylactic surgery, which fortunately turned out all right. When he was in intensive care, back in New York, he assured me over the phone that he wasn't drunk when the accident happened. Obviously this was a very important point for him.

I didn't see Steve often when he was in college, but whenever I was in New York I did a lot of drinking with him. I certainly didn't see anything wrong with that. As long as it was alcohol, my standards and tolerance for the amount that people drank was quite high.

When I remarried years later, I'd been sober in AA for several years and was also attending Al-Anon. We invited my children to come out to California for the wedding. Thom declined, but

Christine and Steve came. My wife and I were cosecretaries of an Al-Anon beginner's group at that time. We asked Steve and Christine if they would like to go to the meeting. My daughter said that she did not need that, but Steve went with us.

During the short course of that meeting, he heard me say things he'd never heard before. I think that during the weekend he spent with us, he probably saw a relationship with my present wife that he had never seen between his mother and me.

When he returned to New York, he decided to go into Alcoholics Anonymous. He stayed sober for a few years, and there was a big change in our relationship. We became more honest and open with each other. We would talk about more meaningful things than we ever did when he was growing up. We began to understand each other as human beings rather than father and son.

Steve also started attending ACA meetings (Adult Children of Alcoholics). His statement to me was, "So much of this goes so deep." I'm sure it was very painful for him.

In addition, both he and Thom had lived with my first wife on and off before they married. She was still drinking. All my children recognized that she had a major problem with alcohol. It presented a special difficulty for Steve. He was working through a lot of issues. A number of years later there was an intervention with my first wife by the three children. She hasn't had a drink since.

Even though I was 3,000 miles away from all this, Steve and I were working a lot of things out. Steve got married. He continued to go to ACA and, as I say, we had a fairly good level of communication.

Then his wife left their marriage. This was very hard on him. I felt some responsibility for that because I hadn't been a very good role-model for how a husband should behave in a marriage. I'm a great one for guilt.

At first Steve stayed sober. He got very close to my daughter and her family. He spent a lot of time with them and had much support from Christine.

Steve experienced three or four years of continuous sobriety. He had a sponsor, but I never met him. I don't know how well Steve did in working through the 12 steps. When he got into the ACA issues, I thought that was important for him. I wanted him to pursue them. I told him, there isn't any question about which is the primary program. A person isn't likely to continue with Al-Anon work if he or she goes back to drinking. That's the bottom line.

Steve did start drinking again. He met a woman in a bar and eventually they started living together. Later on they were married. Fortunately nothing dramatic has happened so far. He's been able to hold down a job, and they bought a house.

A year ago my wife and I were back East on two occasions and we spent time with him at his home. He had made so much progress when he was in AA and ACA, but it isn't that way anymore. He's drinking pretty much how I used to. He'll be working around the house or garden, and constantly has to have a beer in his hand. Just like me in my drinking days, Steve expects everyone to accept him exactly as he is. I drank the way I drank whether or not my mother thought I was drinking too much. It made absolutely no difference. Now he does the same thing.

I've stopped trying to control Steve's drinking. I've said everything I could possibly say about it. I know he's aware. I've told him. I also wrote, telling him that I'm not going to belabor the point anymore, but that I would be less than honest if I didn't tell him that a little voice inside of me keeps screaming, "I wish you'd get yourself back to AA." Otherwise, I haven't interfered in a number of years.

Steve also smokes. He has a horrible cough in the morning. I've lost a sponsor and several relatives and AA friends to lung cancer. It is painful to see him smoking.

I look at him and I can't help but feel responsible. He reminds me so much of myself. This is a classic example of alcoholism as a family disease. Intellectually I know there isn't anything I can do to shortcut what's happening. He knows where Alcoholics Anonymous is. He knows all of the things he was working on in ACA. He just isn't working on them any longer.

Part of me thinks he should know better. He was making some progress in AA. He should know better.

Another consequence of Steve's drinking is that he isn't nearly as close to his sister and her children as he was. He bought a house not too far from Christine but weeks and months pass without their seeing each other. Steve and his wife don't have Christine's family over for get-togethers very often. They go to my daughter's house for Christmas and holidays, but it's a different relationship than it was. Primarily he visits with his drinking friends and his wife's sisters and brothers throughout the eastern part of the country.

Steve and I didn't lose everything when he returned to drinking. It's better than it was before he went into AA. We're a lot more honest with each other. I think Steve has gotten to the point where he trusts me. Still, his drinking does change the relationship.

I don't talk with him about his drinking. He knows how I feel. It's painful to see. I don't know what long-term impact this may have for his marriage. It seems to be working out well for now. I like my second daughter-in-law very much.

For now, at least, Steve is better off than pre-AA, but I don't think he feels he's a social drinker. I'm sure that he has some concern. He's certainly been around long enough to recognize the impact when both of your parents are alcoholics.

Thom

As soon as my oldest son, Thom, started drinking outside the house, he had problems. He had a big mouth and would get into fights in bars. He also had a thing about wrecking automobiles. We lived in a small town in New York State. I worked for a company where alcohol was discouraged, certainly during working hours (lunches and so on). A lot of people who lived in the community worked for the same company I did. It was far from a company town, but there was a good smattering of people who were employed by this particular company. Everybody knew everybody else in town, so Thom's drinking problems were public knowledge and reflected on me.

One evening Thom and a friend of his were crossing the highway near our house. His mother went out and was attempting to persuade him to come home. I think she'd been drinking, and so had Thom. He was trying to take her back across the highway, when the police came along. They didn't know what was going on, so they stopped. Thom, in his usual fashion, told the police it was none of their business. The police came to the house and my youngest son, Steve, got involved, telling them to leave his brother alone and let him go. He was all set to defend his brother. Fortunately, the police knew Steve was a member of the football team, and they just told him to "cool it." One thing led to another and Thom and his friend were taken down to the local police station.

When I went to bail them out, the police wouldn't accept a check so I had to leave Thom and his friend there overnight. The next morning the police didn't require any bail after all. I'm sure they just wanted to keep them until they sobered up. Originally, Thom went to a university in Colorado. He selected it because there was a good school of hotel management, a field in which he was interested.

I drove him across country to school and didn't hear from him again for some time. Eventually, I heard that he'd taken off to go to the Super Bowl in Los Angeles and was gambling in Las Vegas. I brought him home at the end of his first year of college. He'd probably never have graduated at the rate he was going.

One of the things I'd done through all those years was discourage drug use. It was a big topic of conversation at the dinner table. I would tell Thom and his friends that alcohol was legal, and marijuana wasn't. I didn't want to ever hear they were using any of that stuff. I was very upset when Thom was picked up with some of his friends, and they had marijuana in the car. We had to hire a lawyer. I was the only parent who showed up with those four or five kids when they were going before the Justice of the Peace. It was a terrible thing to me. Marijuana—something that was illegal!

Over a period of years after I left my first wife, Thom and I became increasingly estranged. He'd held the divorce against me, and definitely took his mother's side. At Steve's second wedding, Thom refused to come when he learned I would be attending.

Thom married and was divorced. He presently lives with a woman. I believe she's in AA or NA (Narcotics Anonymous). Thom stopped drinking a number of years ago and hasn't resumed as far as I'm aware. I don't know if he's in AA. I ask my other children how he is, but not about his drinking.

Some time ago his current lady friend wrote me a very nice letter, in which she tried to explain Thom's feelings about his mother and me. I understood her concern, but answered her as politely as possible that if Thom had something to say to me, I'd prefer to talk with him directly. Since then, Thom hasn't communicated with me.

Over the years, whenever I was going to be in New York, I always used to let Thom know that I'd like to see him. He never wanted to meet. Eventually, all I was doing was sending him a check on his birthday and at Christmas. I never heard back from him. Finally, one year I decided that one-way communication doesn't work. I let him know that I felt I was interfering in his life and I didn't want to do that. A year later I saw fit to change my attitude, and let him know again that I'd like to see him. He's never responded. Today we're not in communication at all.

Christine

To the best of my knowledge, my daughter Christine's primary problem with alcohol comes from the other side. She hasn't had any obvious difficulties with alcohol use, but she suffers from the effects of the disease just like everyone else. Christine was the overachiever in the family. She's very much in control and everything is very manageable in her life.

I believe Christine needs Al-Anon. However, she's on a fast career track while at the same time raising two children and "doesn't have time."

She is just happy that the intervention on her mother worked— she now has a grandmother for her children. My ex-wife is staying dry without the benefit of AA, and Christine doesn't see any reason she herself needs Al-Anon. After all, the family she grew up in did not believe in ever seeking outside help for anything.

Bottom Line

Today I know I was a very poor model as a husband and father, nor did I provide a good home environment. Alcohol was always too important. It's painful to see the continuing effects of my active alcoholism on my children and know that I'm powerless to remove their resentments or make them well. Only they can do that.

However, I'm a different person now, and I believe my children recognize this. They also know the importance of both AA and Al-Anon in my life. Today I am a better husband and father, and hopefully, a better role-model.

The Heart of a Father

Joining a Family

I have two children, a stepson and an adopted daughter. At the time I came into their lives, Roland was thirteen or fourteen, and Tammy (Tamara) was seven. My wife, Corala, and I met when she was in a treatment program and I was one of the counselors. I was already a recovering alcoholic and addict, so my kids never saw me loaded, not once. That's afforded me a lot of credibility in our family.

With my wife it was different. The kids had seen her high and they'd seen different treatment attempts fail. For years their lives were in turmoil. All those times she was trying to recover, they lived in different relatives' homes.

During treatment the issue of molestation suddenly came up. Tammy had been molested by a man, and it was only then coming to light. There were investigations by CPS workers (Child Protective Services). As a counselor in Corala's treatment program, I came into the picture during the investigations. That's how we met.

Later, Corala and I were married. When I first moved in, it was wonderful. Tamara had never known her father. I was unable to have children and had always wanted a little girl, so it was like a match made in heaven. Tammy's not an addict. She's a good girl who doesn't use drugs.

However, Roland had a real struggle to integrate into the family. He was used to being shuffled around. He was also the one in the family who, when my wife was using, was the caretaker. For all intents and purposes, he was the head of the house. It was hard for him to see this new woman being clean and sober and wanting to do things and not having to leave in the middle of the night. He no longer had to take care of his sister. That was hard for him. He had a real struggle with that.

We had several failed attempts initially, Roland and I, at bonding. He was always very angry. I know now that his issue was, "Who are you and what have you done with my mother?" He expressed that, not clearly, but very angrily. He would say things like, "I don't need you. We don't need you. What are you doing here? You're just another ..." I tried to be soft and gentle and to love him through that process, but he didn't want anything to do with it.

He had so many unresolved issues with his mother. He didn't have a real foundation to accuse me of anything because he'd never seen me loaded. I had only been the "good guy." So he would try to hold in his anger and of course it would blow out in other ways.

About two years into our family's struggle to live together, it was obvious to me that Roland was smoking weed in his room. He was also jumping out the window late at night and going over to some old guy's house to smoke marijuana. When we would ask him about it, he'd deny it.

It was all this stuff I used to do. However, I had the luxury of not having the parental guilt that what he did was my fault. My wife did, though, and we had several struggles around her guilt issues. Actually, the only thing we ever really argued about was Roland and how to parent. Corala was in denial about his smoking.

One day I went into Roland's room and looked around. I found a weed box with his papers in it and some roaches. I confronted my wife. The arguing really escalated. If I hadn't had a sponsor with similar experiences who could share with me his experience, strength, and hope, I would have left. I love my wife intensely, but that wasn't enough. I didn't know what I was getting into when I married into this family.

Even though I'd never had children of my own, I had worked in the field of counseling with adolescents for years. They taught me how to parent. They'd come into my office and say, "My daddy says I can't smoke weed, but he drinks every night. That's not fair." They made total sense. Kids know what they're talking about. They're not stupid.

At that time I was doing a late-night group so I was getting home at about 9:00 P.M. As always, I would come in and there had been some drama in the house. My wife's struggle was, "Hey look! You're making me choose, you or Roland! I'm in the middle. I'm struggling with this. You've got to help me out."

One of those times I decided to sit down and have a talk with Roland. He was high. I could see that look in his eyes. That "I got a secret. You don't know what it is. I'm feeling really good. I'm getting over on you. I'm sitting in your house talking to you while you drink your coffee and I'm blitzed." I could see that in his eyes.

If I had a drug of choice, it would have been marijuana. That's what I did for the longest. I did that from junior high school until the day I got clean. As I talked to Roland, and saw that look on his face, I thought to myself, "You know, you could really enter into relationship with this kid if you smoked a joint with him." As soon as the idea came up I dispelled it. "That's crazy!"

I thought I had dispelled the thought but the next night, coming home from work, I found myself driving through this district where you can buy marijuana. Then all of a sudden it was real to me that this insanity needed to stop—right now. It was about to destroy our family. I was about to get loaded.

In the meantime, Tamara was getting As in school and being the good kid. I wanted to make sure she got as much attention for being good as Roland got for being bad. Even so, Roland was starting to get all my attention and I would give Tammy the leftovers.

When Roland was around seventeen, he came in one night with a pager on. My understanding of pagers at that time was either you were a doctor or you were selling drugs. I questioned him about the pager. Sure enough, he was selling dope. Weed, he said. But I know about kids minimizing, so I suspected he was also selling cocaine.

I demanded that Roland give me the pager. It was the first time that he openly defied me.

He looked at me and said, "I'm not going to give you this. The people I'm hooked up with, you don't want anything to do with them. So I'm protecting you by not letting you get this pager from me."

I didn't even consult with my wife. I told him, "Leave this house. Do it right now. Either give me the pager, or get out." It had gotten to that point.

"Well, can I leave tomorrow?" he asked.

"No. Give me the pager now or leave—now!" I replied.

I went and got some garbage bags. I put all his clothes in the bags and escorted him to the door. He walked down the street dragging his bags. It was just the hardest thing I have ever done. My wife was crying. I felt like such a failure at that time. I wanted to run down the street and say, "Never mind. Never mind, man. Come on, let's smoke that joint."

The God that's in me, the recovery that's in me, wouldn't let me do that, although it was an option that night. I wanted so desperately to have a relationship with this kid. I had asked God, when Corala and I first got married, to give me the heart of a father for this kid. And God did. So although I could disconnect on the guilt level, Roland was truly my son. I hadn't known how hard it was to have the feelings of a father. I could no longer say to my wife, "Well, he's your kid."

As Roland walked down the street carrying his bags, my wife was saying, "When you get home from work tomorrow, I'll be gone if you go through with this." It was almost the last day of my marriage.

I was desperate, but I got some direction from my AA sponsor. It seemed like goofy direction but I followed it because I didn't know what else to do. He told me, "When you drive to work today, don't listen to your radio. Turn all the music off and sing. Remember that song you used to sing when you were a little kid in church—*Yes, Jesus Loves Me*. Sing that all the way to work."

It sounded crazy, but I did it because I didn't know what else to do. I did find peace in the song and I was able to stay at work all day and do my job. When I got back in the car on the way home, the song was still in the car waiting for me, so I sang it all the way home.

When I got home, both Corala and Roland were there. She was telling him, "I don't want to live like this. If you don't stop using, go." And he left.

That was the first time we had ever joined on any kind of discipline, or anything that was related to Roland. Corala had changed. She'd always known that her guilt feelings let Roland get to her, but she wasn't able to get past it. For some reason it got through to her that day. She was very clear, very focused, saying, "You can't stay." So he left.

Since that time, Roland has gone through a lot. He got into a relationship with one of Corala's young sponsees, Diana, who he'd met at an AA meeting. They have a child.

The relationship's been very rocky. Diana's drug of choice was crack cocaine. First Roland would be clean and sober and she wouldn't, then they'd change places. Corala and I had to learn to stay out of their marriage. At one point we threatened to notify Child Protective Services because we didn't want our granddaughter raised in an environment like that. We didn't follow through with the threat. Both Roland and Diana woke up and decided to get clean.

Roland got violent with Diana. She kicked him out of the house and he would repeat his childhood, going from relative's house to relative's house. Doors began to close behind him. He'd do things like steal money from his grandmother's purse. All our relatives are flaming codependents. So it's like, "Steal my money. I didn't see it. I had a hundred dollars in my purse and it's gone now. I must have spent it." Finally they'd close the door and he would go to the next relative—until he had nowhere to go.

He wanted to come back here several times and always our condition was that he not use and that he go into a recovery program. A few times he agreed. He would come home. I'd call someone I knew that worked in a recovery program who would put him at the head of the list. He would get in and stay the weekend and run away again. That happened three or four times. Finally I said, "No, you go to a recovery house first, then you can come home." So he did that and he would go back to Diana. They were always trying to reconcile, but their recoveries were tenuous and temporary.

Roland was always able to lie well. He was just the most charming kid you would ever want to meet. He's got a smile. He knows all the right things to say. His many recovery attempts have taught him the recovery language so he knows how to reel it off.

"One day at a time, Mom, I'm going to make it."

Two years ago at Christmas time Roland came over after all the festivities had ended. I made a point of never giving him cash. My wife was really strapped that year doing Christmas shopping. We weren't expecting him. Corala put some money in a card and gave it to him.

Roland went out and bought some crack, smoked it, and decided he needed some more. So he went to a major shopping center. He had a BB gun. A woman pulled up to a stop sign. He pulled up next to her, pulled the gun out, and took her purse. He got about twelve dollars from her. Then he went down to a smaller mall in the next town, and did the same thing. Then he went to the airport.

He and a friend were smoking crack together in the friend's car. The friend was the wheel man and Roland was the stickup man with the BB pistol. He'd never done anything like this. His disease had progressed.

That night Roland went to jail for three armed robberies. He was sentenced to two years in prison. While he was in prison, he married Diana. She became a Christian, and stopped using. She was a changed person. One day I was driving to work and I saw her in her car. She was also driving to work and she was just praising the Lord, all by herself. She's really changed.

When Roland got out, he and Diana moved in together again. It lasted about two weeks. He started to use again. That's been their story, over and over again. He gets out and gets to the crack pipe. He turns into a different guy.

All the while, Tammy continued to grow. Her mother began spending a lot of time with her and giving her a lot of attention.

I think Roland saw this happening and he was jealous. He begged Corala to let him come home. So we let him come home six months ago. He said he wasn't using. He had a job. He had kept it for a while, which was a new thing. We wanted to help Roland to get back on his feet, so we insisted that he go to some meetings. We told him that if he was going to stay with us, he'd have to be in by a certain time and pay us $50 for food. He's twenty-five, and in some ways we were treating him like he's sixteen. I didn't think he would last long. Sure enough, he didn't.

Roland came home for lunch one day. I was at work. Tammy and Corala were there. My wife asked him for the $50 and he went crazy. He literally tore the house up. He broke things. He ripped the screen door off our front door. He threw plants around and broke mirrors. He threatened my wife physically. Had it not been for my little girl's courage, because she got in between them, Roland could have hit his mother. But Tammy said, "If you hit her, you've got to hit me first."

There's always potential for violence, and that day it came to a head. Corala had asked Roland to be accountable. His response was, "The way I'm living my life is your fault." He left her with such an overwhelming feeling of guilt that when I got home she was crying, "It's my fault." The house was torn up and Tammy was just trembling.

The first thing I wanted to do, because he's a man now, was to find him and beat him up. No one's threatened my wife, come into my house and done this, ever.

Of course I didn't go after him. We got all his stuff and put it outside. He called a few hours later and apologized to me, not his mother, for disrespecting my home. I told him, "I'm calling the police. Come get your clothes. They're under the tree outside."

I called the police. They came over and did a police report. My wife was so riddled with guilt that she lied to the police about what happened. She stammered, "Well no, he didn't really ... I think he may have tripped on his way out and that's why the door ... I don't think it was..."

But Tammy said, "Mamma, no!" in front of the police. "No, he can't do that and come back here."

Tammy does really well in terms of keeping her Mom honest. We finally got the truth out. The police went to Roland's job and arrested him. He was still on parole, but I didn't press charges. So they held him, I think seventy-two hours, and let him go.

I didn't press charges because of Corala. If it had been just me, I would have done it. Initially Corala said, "Don't call the police." If it hadn't been for my anger, I probably wouldn't have. When the officer told us we needed to decide whether to press charges within seventy-two hours, I just decided that I wouldn't do that, without praying about it or anything.

I regret that decision. I'm really glad that Roland went to jail. He didn't come over here again until about a month ago, when he finally apologized to his mother and his sister.

I gave him a bill. "This is what you broke. This is how much it cost." So it's yet up in the air. His parole agent told him that he needed to go to a drug program, but they're not really enforcing it. It's more like a suggestion. They've told him, though, "Another drug related offense and you're going back to prison."

He's not into three strikes yet. At one point he said he was going to go to a drug program, but of course he hasn't gone.

Now the holidays are here and it's family time so all those issues come up for us. He didn't come over on Thanksgiving, but he was welcome. I believe Corala let him know he could. He could spend Christmas day with us, too. But we are united that he will never live here again. He'll just have to go to jail or be homeless.

Roland has so many unresolved issues. They've escalated over the years and he is so bitter. He's very angry under all that charm. He masks it well, but when he explodes, each explosion gets more and more detrimental to everyone else around him. He's acting up physically. My fear is that he will harm Corala, even though he's riddled with guilt for what he did to her and really does love her a lot. Or he could harm himself, because he can be suicidal, too.

My position is that he's a grown man and he has to make his own decisions. Although it's really difficult to watch, he can do whatever he wants to do. He just doesn't get to do it here. Corala and I are working on developing a joint boundary system. When Roland's acting out, he can't come here.

Although Corala's much healthier than she was years ago, Roland still knows where her guilt switch is. It's really hard to watch, but it doesn't come between us like it once did. We are united in that it's clear he's an addict and he needs recovery and he can't come here. I'm OK with that.

When I see him affecting my life even at long distance, over the phone, however, I go back to that place of rage. A fear for me has been that, at some point, Roland and I will get physical together. That hasn't happened yet. He's a big man now, bigger than he was. His disease has progressed to where he probably thinks, "I can beat you up." Maybe he could. I don't know. I definitely don't want that to happen.

In the meantime, Tammy will be starting college and is doing really, really well. She's made a lot of healthy decisions around boyfriends. She won't go out with anybody that uses or smokes weed, even in their spare time, let alone get in the car with somebody that's under the influence. I'm sure she's been affected by watching all this drama around Roland. I'm going to miss her terribly.

For many years I've been helped by an African American men's group I helped start, of recovering alcoholics and addicts. The group began by addressing our issues of anger. It has become a Christian, married men's support group where everybody is in recovery.

Today I feel safe. I don't have to worry about coming home from work and finding Roland there on the couch. I feel pretty confident about that. I also feel good that we have been able to forgive him. I did a teaching about forgiveness not too long after he trashed our house. I learned a lot from that. We had a family meeting, Corala, Tammy, and I, around forgiveness and how it wasn't the same thing as amnesia. But we could forgive him.

I know what it's like to be at that place where you're just about to succeed, and then sabotage yourself. I lived much of my life like that. I can totally relate to Roland. He's got that secondary denial. He knows he's an addict but he doesn't think he needs any help.

I have compassion for him. I just don't like what he does. As long as he doesn't do it around me, I can stay in this compassionate place and be prayerful and forgive him.

On the Road to Serenity

Mother Surmounts Clashing Cultures

My husband, Roy, and I are both Hispanic immigrants. He's been in the United States since he was three. My family came when I was a teenager. Roy is a recovering alcoholic in Alcoholics Anonymous. We have two children. Billy, the oldest, is twenty-five. His sister, Tina, is three years younger, and married. My eighty-three-year-old mother lives with us.

I first noticed Billy was using marijuana when he was about thirteen and I was cleaning his room. I really got shaken up. I called my husband. We didn't know what to do. My husband's first reaction was to take Billy to the police department to scare him. The police told Billy that if he did that again, they were going to put him in Juvenile Hall. I don't think they would have, but the scare worked. I never caught anything else in the house. Billy looked normal to me.

Still, he kept the same friends across the street, who had given him marijuana in the first place. My husband and I told Billy, "We don't want you to have those friends. You're going to get yourself in trouble."

Billy announced we couldn't choose his friends. Then he started getting bad grades, Fs and Ds. We talked with the teachers, and arranged that for every class he would bring a piece of paper from the teacher saying Billy had attended that class. Even so, he wasn't doing too good. At that point I think as parents we tried the best we could and the best we knew how, to deal with Billy.

Pretty soon the same pattern started, with the school calling to say he had missed classes. I tried to be a peacemaker. I knew in my heart that Billy wasn't going the right way, but I didn't want to tell my husband because he took things really hard and lost his temper.

One day, when Billy was about sixteen, the teacher called.

"Mrs. Santos, is something wrong with Billy? He never comes to school any more."

"What? He's been going to school every day."

"No, Mrs. Santos, he has missed twenty-one days."

"Oh my God! How come I didn't know about this?"

"Billy's been bringing signed excuses," replied his teacher, "saying you've been signing them."

"No! I never sign notes for Billy not to go to school."

We found out Billy had been playing hooky at a cousin's. We didn't know why he did that. The principal of the school said, "Well, it's either of two things, sex or drugs."

"I don't know about sex, they're first cousins," Roy and I thought. "Maybe it *is* drugs." And that's what it was. This cousin's husband was involved with a lot of drugs.

When Billy was a younger teenager, we used to have open dialogues with our kids. We'd pick one day a week, maybe a Sunday. Each one of us would bring up whatever we wanted. We'd talk about drugs, about school, about being careful.

We were always doing things together with our kids. It's not like we ignored Billy and Tina. We went on vacation to Hawaii twice. We visited the old country for five weeks. Billy and Tina went everywhere with us. We all did things together.

Billy was a very closed child. Tina communicates a lot, but not Billy. I knew he had plenty inside. My husband used to lay down the law. "OK, Billy. You have to go to school. You have to be able to get a good job," and so on. But Billy's grades kept going down.

One day we made Billy go to the doctor for a blood test because Roy and I needed to know what was going on. They found he had some cocaine in his blood, so he was doing not just marijuana, but cocaine, too.

We didn't know where Billy got his money. I started noticing that some money was missing from my purse. Twenty dollars would be gone. But I was so naive that I thought, "Did I lose it? Did I buy something?"

Finally I figured it out. It had to be Billy.

"Billy, did you take any money from me?" I asked him.

It was a dumb question. Of course he wasn't going to admit it.

Billy got all upset. "Mom, what do you think, I'm stealing money from you? No! Be sensible."

You just don't imagine this is going to happen in your family until it really knocks at your door. When I finally realized the truth, I didn't say anything to Roy. In those days he was still drinking. I was scared of his temper, so I kept a lot inside me. Keeping things inside is bad. I was hurting and not getting any help.

149

When Billy was about sixteen, we heard of Al-Anon. I used to hear about AA, but not Al-Anon. I would think, "Go to something, get some help." But then I'd say to myself, "Things will pass. Billy's young. He's going to go to school and graduate. All kids go through these things."

But he didn't go to school and he didn't graduate.

Billy started getting close to graduation. He was still doing bad in school. Then he told me one day, "I want to quit school."

I said, "What? You're so close to graduation! You can't quit school."

He insisted, "I want to quit. I can't make it and graduate."

The three of us, Roy, Billy, and I, talked to the principal, who said, "Billy, you can make it. You're smart. If you really get into these books, you can do it."

But Billy had his mind made up.

In the country where I grew up, you have to go to school, and you have to finish. But here, I guess, by sixteen or whatever, you aren't required to continue high school. Billy quit six months before graduation. We did everything we could, but Billy didn't want to do anything.

We told him, "OK, Billy, if you're not going to go to school, you have to go to work. I'm sorry, but you're not staying in this house without working. Go get some job applications." Billy would pick up some applications, then never fill them out. We had huge arguments because he wouldn't go to work. He wasn't in school. We were getting so frustrated. We didn't know how to deal with this problem with Billy. We couldn't understand what was going on.

I always had hopes for Billy. Roy, who was still drinking, would see the worst part of Billy, and I would only see the good part. I was positive that Billy would change. My husband would say, "He's not going to change." We had terrible arguments. At this point our marriage was not good. It was on the rocks, in fact.

"Maybe we should sell this house," we thought. "Move. Get new friends. If Billy gets away from his neighborhood friends, maybe he will change." It's always that hope that you have for your child.

Billy would answer, "Well, drugs are all over the place."

We decided anyway to sell the house and move to a beautiful new area. Billy continued to do his same thing. Finally he found a job. He was a very good worker and the company liked him. But getting him up in the morning was so much frustration. He lost his job because he became irresponsible.

I'm very involved with the Hispanic community and my church. I'm a reader at services. I sing in the Hispanic choir. Billy was an altar boy. My husband was involved with the Council, too. We had a good environment for our children. I'd look around at all our friends and think, "My God, I envy them. They have kids the same age as Billy, and those kids have cars and jobs and their lives together. Billy's not doing anything."

The girls liked Billy, but he wasn't ever serious about one. Sometimes I really wished that he had a girlfriend.

"If he had a nice girl," I thought, "he'd have a responsibility. He'd be sharing something with somebody. I don't even care if they move in together."

Now where I came from, you get married first, and you get married in church by the priest. Then you move in together. Before you're married, you have to have a chaperone. It's very strict. I always believed in those customs. But by that time I was so frustrated I didn't care if Billy found a girl and moved in with her. Unfortunately that never happened.

I was obsessed with Billy. I was wrapped up in his problems. Roy got sober and began to change for the better, but I was so obsessed with Billy that I hardly noticed.

Billy just got worse. He lived with relatives, then he'd move back in with us for two or three days, take a shower, sleep, and take off again. He was stealing things. My husband gave me a beautiful keyboard which I kept in the closet. I love music and play by ear. One day I went to the closet and the keyboard was gone. My heart just broke in so many places.

Billy phoned.

"Billy, did you steal my keyboard?" I asked. He didn't say anything.

"That's it! I don't want to hear any more excuses!" I raged. "You can't come back here until you bring my keyboard."

Billy stayed away for awhile. He knew from experience that I'd calm down, and he could come back and lie around on the couch and let me take care of him. So that's what he did. He knew how to push my buttons.

But Roy'd had it. One day he called me at work and said, "I just threw Billy out of the house. I don't want him here anymore."

"How could you!" I yelled. "This house is mine, too." I just went crazy. I was so mad at Roy. I cried all the time and I couldn't sleep. I was ready to leave Roy.

We went to see a counselor. We had decided to split up. Somehow, though—I don't know how—we got back together. We sat down and said, "We either can do this or we can talk to each other every day." So now we sit down and spend time with each other every day, and let our feelings out. Little by little we built our marriage up again.

We didn't see Billy for a long time. I blamed myself and my husband for Billy's problems. I felt so ashamed. In the old country, you're always supposed to take care of your kids, no matter what. Our relatives all tried to help Billy with jobs and a place to stay, but nothing worked. By now he was twenty-five and on crack.

A friend who's a priest told Roy and me to look for some help. We went to Toughlove for five months. Peoples' stories made me a little stronger.

Then Billy was picked up by the police for riding a bike someone else had stolen. Soon afterwards we helped him buy a car so he could find a job. He didn't find one, and he had no insurance on the car. He hit somebody with the car. He was arrested and sent to jail. I thought I would die from fear and the disgrace.

One night, friends knocked at our door. Billy had been injured jumping with his mountain bike up in the hills, probably high on drugs. He crushed a heel in six places. His friends brought him home because he had nowhere else to go. Roy didn't want him in the house, but we got him medical attention and I took care of him for several weeks. All the time I hoped and prayed that now Billy would come to his senses.

The priest visited and talked to him. "Billy, God is trying to tell you something. He's trying to tell you to stop!" It went in one ear and out the other.

As Billy's heel got better, he went back to his old ways of lying around and watching TV. But I had begun to change. I love Billy, yet I felt like banging his head against the wall.

I started to nag. "Pick up after yourself. Wash your plate. Don't leave things around for your grandma." She's in pretty good shape, but I don't want her to be doing things for Billy that he can do for himself. She loves him so much that she feels sorry for him and lets him back in the house when Roy and I aren't here.

I should have gone to Al-Anon a long time ago. Our priest told me, "Maria, you need to go to Al-Anon. If one meeting doesn't suit you, if you don't feel comfortable, just try another one." I couldn't understand that I needed to change. I never understood that Billy had an illness.

Finally, I was desperate enough to try Al-Anon. Tina and Roy go with me sometimes. I'm no longer a marshmallow. I'm getting tougher, and Roy's getting calmer. I've learned I have a tremendous amount of anger. Recently I got really angry with Billy for not following through once more on something he had promised to do for me. He had come home and I saw him lying on the couch. I was ready to explode. My husband said, "Maria, say the Serenity Prayer."

"I already said it three times! It's not working," I cried.

A couple of days later I started to boil over again. So I went in the garage and said the Serenity Prayer. After that I felt like something commanded me, "Relax, Maria. I'll take care of that. Don't worry." And I calmed right down.

I have so much anger in me. I want to change that. I want to have serenity, not anger. I think it'll take a few years. But Al-Anon says, "Keep coming back." And I will because I want to have serenity more than anger in me.

A Marriage Encounter group that we've belonged to for three years has helped us a lot with Billy, and with Roy's and my problems. We meet once a month. It's a very close group. When we're down, they lift us up. When others get down, we lift them up.

You always dream good things about your kids. I don't want to give up. I'm the kind of person who's very positive about everything. But I think Billy needs to hit bottom really bad, maybe, to change.

Now I'm taking one day at a time dealing with this problem. I've been in Al-Anon only four months, not too long. In listening to other people I have begun to understand that I'm not alone. You know, there's other people worse off than me. I was finally ready to listen.

My faith is very important to me. I believe God does things for a purpose, maybe to help someone along the line. Through our pain, and now hope for ourselves, maybe we can help some other parents.

Generation unto Generation

A Grandfather Tells His Story

My father was a drunk. My male relatives all passed away from drinking. They got sick. Kidneys started failing, whatever. My father had ulcers. He died from cancer, but the last year of his life he was drinking twenty-four hours a day. He drank from the time I was born. I used to hate it when he was drunk. I was never going to be like him. When he was sober, I loved him. He changed when he was drinking. I can remember that when I was a kid, he spent all his money.

I wanted to run the house, more or less. I was just a kid trying to help my mother. I grew up that way. When I got older and my father was still alive, I started drinking and I got worse than he was. Then he would hide from me. I didn't know anything until I got sober. Then I wished everybody was sober.

My parents were immigrants from Mexico. All the Mexican people in my town lived in the same neighborhood. There's no particular stigma for men alcoholics, but there used to be a lot of stigma for any Mexican women alcoholics.

I have three sons and three daughters. My daughters have no problem with alcohol. They just don't drink. They could probably take one and it wouldn't bother them, but they don't even do that.

My oldest daughter has a son who's into drugs and alcohol, though. I talk to him, but he's in denial. I think he's already burned from taking too many drugs. He was going to college. He started when he was seventeen, but he didn't pass all the classes. His grades went down. As a matter of fact, he started forgetting what he had learned.

It's hard to make him see it. He's got different thinking. He tells everybody he eats all kinds of mushrooms or whatever. He tries all kinds of drugs. He's not ashamed to say that he did it. My daughter feels really bad about it because she's working and they put aside $50,000 to send him to college. Then this happens. He doesn't think anything about it. Now he's selling shoes. What can I say? He knows.

I've been trying to convince my daughter to go to Al-Anon, but she hasn't yet.

My second oldest daughter's husband is a drunk. She has three children and a grandson—my great-grandson. He's about three.

My sons are another story. All three are alcoholics, but they're not into drugs. They're the wrong generation for drugs. Even when I was drinking, I didn't have too much of a hard time with my sons. I used to get after them, though. I'd tell the youngest one, Pete, not to go to Sears on the bicycle. The traffic was too dangerous. I caught him one day, coming from Sears on a bike. He didn't think I'd do anything. Everyone was home. I took him to the garage. I got the belt, but I wasn't hitting him. I was hitting the floor but the other ones were listening. Pete would yell, "You're killing me, Daddy, you're killing me!"

Pete has worked for a contractor for eighteen years. He works and he has his good times. He still drinks and does his own thing. He used to be in trouble with alcohol. He got into arguments at football games. He had to go to a class because of his drinking. The man Pete works for has been sober a long time, so maybe he's a good influence on Pete even though my son hasn't stopped drinking.

Frederick is my oldest son. Five years ago I bailed him out of jail. He married twice. First, he just lived with a girlfriend for about five years. Then they separated. They never had any kids. He got officially married to another woman, again for about five years, and was divorced.

His ex-wife started going to AA and he did, too. He says he was sober for two years.

I talked to Frederick's ex-wife and supported her decision to divorce. I told her the truth. If they couldn't get along, what's the use in living with each other? There's no use getting drunk over this. So they were divorced.

Not too long ago Frederick remarried, this time to an alcoholic. She was also under medication because she would go into convulsions. She drank around the clock. She was passing out in the kitchen. They had a baby, but the marriage didn't last, not even two years. My son asked for a divorce and tried to get custody of the child. They each have the boy three days a week.

They sold the house they'd had for only a year. Frederick bought a mobile home. That's where he's living now. At first he was taking care of himself. One day he went to a party and they didn't have the Coke that he wanted, so he just said, "Give me a beer." So he started drinking again. That's what he tells me. He went back to drinking. Then he got caught drunk driving. He doesn't do drugs, but he still drinks. He goes out in his boat. He and his friends like to fish and drink. I used to do a lot of that when I was drinking, too. It's fun to be out there. He's living his life again the way he wants to. He's still drinking and going out and having a party.

I've never seen Frederick really drunk myself, but I know that he drinks when I'm not around. None of my sons drinks when I'm around. As a matter of fact they hide their bottles or whatever they have when they see me coming. If they're having their own party, I let them have it. I stay away. I don't have any business there.

I don't think they're going to stop because I stopped drinking. If they ever get in trouble, they know what to do. I do tell them a lot of times, "You can't be driving under the influence of alcohol." Whether they like it or not, I still bring it up. But that's all I say. Then I feel better. It's like telling your child to be careful crossing the street.

Once in a while Pete or Frederick tell me, "I'm going to go check AA out with you one of these days, Dad." Whenever they don't feel too good, I guess. I know that worrying doesn't help. I learned that already. I know how alcoholics think.

Tony is my middle son. He's been clean and sober eighteen years. He's divorced and has three grown sons of his own. Who knows if they've got addictive disease? They're really nice kids. His ex-wife is the daughter of good friends of mine in the AA program. She's not an alcoholic. She and Tony were divorced ten or fifteen years ago now. He had been sober for about three years at that time.

At first I didn't know Tony was an alcoholic. He tells me he and his brothers used to come and "borrow" money from me when I was at work, so they could go buy beer. I was into my own drinking, and thought they were at school. They didn't tell me they were in trouble.

Later on, Tony would black out. After I sobered up, I bought him a car so he could get a job. I just lent it to him before I gave it to him, so I could see how he was going to behave. I hadn't even got through giving it to him when he got drunk and smashed it into a telephone pole with his cousin, and then he came running home. The police nabbed him, but they said, "Let your father take care of you." And they let him go. He totaled the whole car.

I was in AA, but I didn't see that I had no power over Tony. I worried, "What can I do? I can't be with him all the time!"

One day Tony called me and said to come and pick him up. He wanted to go to a meeting with me, so I took him to a few meetings. I thought maybe he was just playing around. I didn't take him seriously. He didn't look as sick as I had been. He just decided that he'd had enough. Every time he drank he'd black out. Then he started going to AA on his own. His in-laws, who were in AA, helped him a lot. He tells me he didn't have to take the beating I did. He came in when he was twenty-three years old. He was able to stop early. He didn't wait until he was forty-some years.

We're always talking. We share a lot of recovery tapes. He goes to meetings whenever he feels like it now. Tony works hard at trying to help other people. He wants to get the whole world sober, all his friends he runs into. He can't get anybody sober. He just thinks he can. I say, "No, no, all you can do is tell them your story."

I haven't seen either Frederick or Pete act the way I used to. They do drink, but the next day they get up and go to work. They work every day. Maybe they say, "Oh I'm not as bad as my dad." The truth is, they're in denial. They want to keep on drinking.

In AA you're finally grateful to be sober. It's been with God's help all the way. I haven't had any heart problems since I sobered up. I didn't want to stay sick. My life has turned around and I make what I want to make out of it. And it's always changing!

Wow! We're a Family!

A Fourth Chance Miracle
for a Single Mother

I have two teenage daughters, Ann and Tanesha, and a ten-year-old son, James. I'm a single mother, never married. Each of my kids has a different father. All of the fathers are alcoholics. One daughter knows her father. The other two children don't.

Because of my alcoholism, I gave away my kids three times. The legal system didn't make me. I just had a moment of clarity where I didn't want my kids to see me as a drunk. The disease had progressed so that I didn't feel like taking them to school any more or even doing the basic, necessary things everyday—you know, combing their hair and cooking meals. I couldn't keep a job. I couldn't maintain a household. So I gave them away to my parents and sisters three times.

My parents live in a very nice area. They are very religious. My mom's a missionary and my dad's a deacon. I was raised in the church so I didn't know much about drinking, but I would see it on Sundays with my father's brothers and sisters. When I was growing up, drinking looked like fun. I never saw violence or sadness with drinking. On my father's side, all of them worked. They were functional alcoholics.

My parents and my sisters became my children's surrogate parents. The kids had their own rooms at my parents' house. They had a structure. They went to school. They were A students. They were well-dressed. They were outstanding, achieving children.

When they finally came back to live with me, it was hard for all of us. I couldn't afford the things my parents could. We had to live in small quarters. At first we were in a studio apartment, all of us. I had to relearn how to take care of my own children.

Everything changed. They stopped going to church on Sunday since I wasn't a church-going person. I had a lot of resentments toward the church because I was brought up so strictly. Although I do have a Higher Power that I choose to call God. Since I don't go to a building to praise God, my parents assume that I don't have a God in my life. Sometimes I tell my mom, "I pray. God hears my prayers." She believes I should at least tell my children to go to church so they'll have that religious background. I do remember the lessons in the Bible. It stopped me a lot of times when I was drinking. As I've gotten older I've fallen back on all those teachings that I had growing up in the church. Now I feel my son, and my daughters, and my granddaughter, should have that, too.

We went from the studio to a homeless shelter until I could afford a bigger apartment. From the homeless shelter we moved to a one-bedroom place. The landlord was charging me $675. The apartment was so small. There was a lot of friction between us. That's when I really found out Ann and Tanesha were drinking. They had to share a room, two teenagers and one little boy.

At that time, I had my boyfriend living with me. My mom told me not to move men into my house with the kids until we're ready to marry—it confuses the kids. Sometimes my mom and I don't agree but this time I listened. I don't move men into my house anymore. That was bad behavior and it affected my children.

When we finally qualified for housing, we got a three-bedroom house. I live there today with my children.

My children had seen what I was like as an alcoholic and an addict and they had some fears about my being clean and sober this last time. They didn't believe it. Their behavior changed around me. They started acting out, like running away.

I first noticed my daughters had a problem with alcohol five years ago, when I was two-and-a-half years sober. I had just got my children back for the fourth time from living with my parents. Ann and Tanesha were about twelve and ten. The girls were into alcohol but I guess I didn't want to see that part.

As they got older, Ann's and Tanesha's behavior changed even more. They were hanging around the wrong group of kids. I don't know exactly when they started drinking, but I could tell from their behavior. I remember what it's like dealing with the peer pressure my kids are going through now—the concerts, the gangs, and the boyfriends.

Every time they want to go to a party I say, "You know I'm going to tell you not to drink. Please don't get drunk. Don't take drugs. I know you do it, but I wish you wouldn't. Respect my house. Don't bring stuff in here."

A couple of times I've found alcohol bottles in their room when I cleaned. Hiding bottles brought up a lot of old feelings for me. First of all, I poured the liquor out. When the kids came home, I confronted them.

"I found these alcohol bottles. I asked you not to bring alcohol into the house. You're messing with my sobriety and you're going to have to move and get your own house if you keep it up."

I laid down other rules, including a curfew. The girls were teenagers and they were rebellious. They would go to their friends and they would come home drunk. A couple of times I found Ann very drunk when I came home from a meeting. I was really angry. She had passed out and vomited. I wanted to clean her up, but I didn't. I thought that if I cleaned her up, I would be implying, "It's OK to be drunk. I'll clean you up." She was horrified that I left her in her own vomit. I reminded her that I had told her not to come home drunk.

Sometimes the girls would sneak alcohol, thinking I didn't know about their drinking. A couple of times I came in after an AA meeting and there were young men in my house. They were all smoking pot and drinking. I was furious. "You want to take my sobriety away! You want me to start drinking again. You want me to be that alcoholic that doesn't care for you!"

I just totally lost it. I had to call my AA sponsor. People in the fellowship came and we aired out the house.

Sometimes I worked out of town at fairs. One time I was working for a fair and my kids had a party in the house. There was drinking. Stuff got stolen. Ann ran away because she thought I would get really angry, that kids just trashed the house. I *was* angry. We had to go for counseling. I worked the steps on that with my sponsor because I was so angry that my children would do something like this. It was really devastating.

My area has a counseling center for single parents who can't deal with their kids' behavior. The counseling turned out to be a plus. I had to go, too. I found out a lot of things about myself as well as about my children. For example, my children have issues about their fathers. And I learned how an alcoholic like myself attracts other alcoholics.

It's hard handling kids. Tanesha is eighteen and has a child herself. I don't want my granddaughter to fall into the pattern of being an alcoholic or an addict as she grows up. I'm trying to stop the cycle with my own children.

When I had about a year of sobriety in AA, I went to Al-Anon because of the man in my life. Al-Anon was really emotional for me. I would go to different meetings. I started hearing what parents, friends, and children go through seeing their loved ones in addiction. They can't save them because they're not ready. The people I listened to didn't go to Al-Anon for themselves, they went for someone else.

But once you come to the program of Alcoholics Anonymous or Al-Anon, a seed is planted. You hear something. At some level, you know what you need to do. Maybe you can't find the words to describe the feeling, but it's there and you remember these people when you stop going. You remember the hugs, and "Keep coming back," and "We're going to love you until you love yourself."

I also belong to a women's group. We're African-American women engaged in a healing process around issues we have from the past. Issues of growing up in a white society, what society says we should be like, how society perceives us to be; strong, domineering, and so on. Well, we're really soft inside, you know. I've met so many people that have helped me during all this.

My oldest daughter is now sharing her feelings with me and talking about her relationships. I talk with her about practicing safe sex and about AIDS. I'm trying to build trust between us and it's hard. I don't want her to be so devastated about something I do or say, that she has to take a drink.

This past year my children have been pushing me to help them find their fathers. Ann and James have medical problems, so I really need to find out their medical background. Ann has severe scoliosis and will probably need a pipe in her back. James was hit by a car when he was seven and is dyslexic. A lot of tragedies have happened to my kids. I talk to Ann about drinking, because she's sickly all the time. It scares me when she drinks. I'm especially concerned about her. She's only fifteen. I don't want her to get caught up in alcohol and drugs. I'm afraid, and I try to shelter her.

Sometimes when she hangs out with a certain group of people, she starts drinking. They're right around the corner from the house. I tell her, "Ann, I know you're drinking. Please don't. You can't afford it. You take medication. I'm really scared."

But lately, because she's bored, she's been going around the corner. She wants to drive, but she isn't old enough yet. She can't get a job. She ran my phone bill to $390. I took her pager because of my phone bill. She was angry, but I told her, "You need to pay my phone bill. I'll keep it until I feel that you are ready." She's been drinking this summer. It's scary. "Come on, Higher Power," I say to myself, "help me. Let's work the steps."

Until school begins again in a few weeks, my solution is to take a couple of hours off from work every day in order to spend more time with Ann. When she's with me, she doesn't drink. That's good. Some days I take her and James to matinees that I can afford. The two hours that I take out of my day are worth it. She doesn't even think about going around the corner. It's like we've been best pals for the last two weeks. As soon as I slack off from those two hours out of the day, she'll start sneaking around the corner. I have to sacrifice my job to do this for my children, but I don't mind. I have a management position where I can make the time up. Those two hours are more precious than money or a job.

Tanesha, the oldest, doesn't drink that much anymore. She works where I do. I got her a job there. She's doing the single-mom routine, but in a different way from me when I was drinking. She wants to cut that pattern off.

At one time I had to be on welfare. However, I wasn't going to live off welfare any longer than I had to. My mom paid for my education so that I could get a job. I didn't want to be in the welfare system. When Tanesha was drinking, I refused to let her live in my house on welfare. She was really angry with me.

"What are you doing?" I asked. "Why do you want to be on welfare? You can get up. You can go to school. You've got two arms and two legs. You're able to go to work."

"Well, how am I going to get there?" she asked. "I don't want to catch the bus with my baby."

So I bought her a car instead of buying a car for myself. It's a nice compact car. It has insurance. Tanesha's been responsible ever since. She goes to work. She's entered community college. She tells me next year she'll be moving out.

Today I'm there for each of my children. I wasn't there before. They really believe they helped me with my recovery. The first two years when they came to live with me, they thought it was just temporary. They had watched me relapse before. When they see me get to that point, they say, "You need to go to a meeting." A couple of times I took Ann to a meeting and she liked it. Also, there were pool tables and pinball machines at the Alano Club. People were having fun. So AA is attracting my daughter.

Tanesha talks to me more. She's being more responsible, a productive member of society. She's finding out that drinking and partying is not all that it claims to be.

I just take one day at a time right now. My son is going through medical problems again and it's really trying me. Because of the accident, he's tired a lot.

But, you know, sometimes when we're all sitting in the living room watching TV, I say, "Wow! We're a family."

PART IV APPENDIX

Following is a selected list of organizations and resources that may be helpful. You will find many other useful resources in libraries, bookstores, the phone book, at 12-step meetings, and from the U.S. Superintendent of Documents at (202) 512-1800. A very good comprehensive catalog-order resource is the Hazelden Foundation, Center City, MN (800) 328-0098.

Resources

Organizations

Adult Children of Alcoholics—See your local phone book.

Al-Anon and Alateen—See your local phone book or call (800) 344-2666.

Alcoholics Anonymous—See your local phone book or call (212) 870-3400.

American Medical Association (County and State)—Ask for referrals to Addictionologists or specialists in addictive disease.

American Society of Addiction Medicine (ASAM)—National Office: (301) 656-3920.

Battered Women's Shelters—See your local phone book.

Codependents Anonymous (CODA)— See your local phonebook.

County Alcohol and Drug Treatment Programs—See your local phone book.

Emotions Anonymous—See your local phone book.

Employee Assistance Programs—See your employer.

Families Anonymous—for families and friends concerned about the use of drugs and alcohol or related behavioral problems. P.O. Box 3475, Culver City, CA 90231-3475. (310) 313-5800. 1-800-736-9805.

Hospital Alcohol and Drug Treatment Programs—Call your local hospital for information.

Narcotics Anonymous—See your local phone book or call (818) 780-3951.

National Alliance for the Mentally Ill (NAMI)—Call (703) 524-7600 or (800) 950-6264.

National Council on Alcoholism and Drug Dependence (NCADD)— See your local phone book for your regional office, or call (212) 206-6770. They have extensive information about local treatment centers and recovery programs.

Parents Anonymous—See your local phone book or call (909) 621-6184.

Parents Letting Go—See Al-Anon.

Professional Counselors (Psychologists, Social Workers, Clergy, School)—Ask them first about their training and experience in addictive disease.

Rational Recovery—See your local phone book, or call (916) 621-4374.

Secular Organizations for Sobriety/Save Our Selves (SOS)—See your local phone book, or call (716) 834-2921.

Suicide Prevention Hotline—See your local phone book or call 911.

Toughlove ®—See your local phone book or call (800) 333-1069.

Veterans Affairs (VA) Hospitals, Clinics, and Vet Centers—See your local phone book under U.S. Government Offices.

Women for Sobriety (WFS)—See your local phone book, or call (215) 536-8026.

Bibliography

Adult Children of Alcoholics

A Time to Heal: The Road to Recovery for Adult Children of Alcoholics. Timmen L. Cermak, M.D. Jeremy P. Tarcher, Inc. Los Angeles. 1988.

It Will Never Happen to Me. Claudia Black. Ballentine Books, Reissue Edition. New York. 1991.

Recovery Library for Acoas. Janet Woititz. Health Communications. Deerfield Beach, FL. 1990.

Alcoholism

Ad·dic·tion·ary: A Primer of Recovery Terms and Concepts from Abstinence to Withdrawal. Jan R. Wilson and Judith A. Wilson. Hazelden Foundation. Center City, MN. 1992.

Alcoholics Anonymous: The Story of How Many Thousands of Men and Women Have Recovered from Alcoholism. Third Edition. Alcoholics Anonymous World Services, Inc. New York. 1976.

Alcoholics Anonymous Comes of Age: A Brief History of A.A. Seventh Printing. Alcoholics Anonymous World Services, Inc. New York. 1977.

Drugfree: A Unique, Positive Approach to Staying Off Alcohol and Other Drugs. Richard B. Seymour and David E. Smith, M.D. Facts on File Publications. New York. 1987. (Also may be ordered from Haight Ashbury Publications, 409 Clayton St., San Francisco, CA 94117.)

Research on Alcoholics Anonymous: Opportunities and Alternatives. Barbara S. McCrady and William R. Miller, Eds. Rutgers Center of Alcohol Studies. New Brunswick, NJ. 1993.

Staying Sober: A Guide for Relapse Prevention. Terence T. Gorski and Merlene Miller. Independence Press. Independence, MO. 1986.

The American Way of Life Need Not Be Hazardous to Your Health. John W. Farquhar, M.D. W.W. Norton and Company. New York. 1978.

Treating the Alcoholic: A Developmental Model of Recovery. Stephanie Brown. John Wiley and Sons. New York. 1985.

Codependency

Against the Wall: Men's Reality in a Codependent Culture. John Hough and Marshall Hardy. Hazelden Foundation. Center City, MN. 1991.

Co-Dependence: Misunderstood—Mistreated. Anne Wilson Schaef. Harper & Row. San Francisco. 1986.

Codependent No More. Melodie Beattie. Hazelden Foundation. Center City, MN. 1996.

Families

Courage to Be Me—Living with Alcoholism. Al-Anon Family Group Headquarters. Virginia Beach, VA. 1996.

How Al-Anon Works for Families and Friends of Alcoholics. Al-Anon Family Group Headquarters. New York. 1995.

Dual Diagnosis

Taking Care of Yourself When a Family Member Has Dual Disorders. Dennis Daley and Janet Sinberg. Hazelden Foundation. Center City, MN. 1989.

When Self-Help Isn't Enough: Overcoming Addiction and Psychiatric Disorders. A. Scott Winter, M.D. Hazelden Foundation. Center City, MN. 1990.

Intervention

I'll Quit Tomorrow: A Practical Guide to Alcoholism Treatment. Revised Edition. Vernon E. Johnson. Harper & Row. San Francisco. 1980.

Intervention: How to Help Someone Who Doesn't Want Help: A Step-by-Step Guide for Families of Chemically Dependent Persons. Vernon E. Johnson Institution. Minneapolis, MN. 1989.

The Times of My LIfe. Betty Ford with Chris Chase. Harper & Row. New York. 1978.

Training Families to Do an Intervention: A Professional's Guide. Johnson Institute. Minneapolis, MN. 1996.

Multicultural Issues

African–Americans in Treatment: Dealing with Cultural Differences. Tommie M. Richardson and Brenda A. Williams. Hazelden Foundation. Center City, MN. 1990.

Multi–cultural Issues. National Association of Alcoholism and Drug Abuse Counselors. Arlington, VA. 1989-1992.

Nicotine Addiction

Combined Tobacco and Alcohol Addictions: A Prototypic Form of Polydrug Abuse. Joan A. Christen and Arden G. Christen. Indiana University School of Dentistry. Indianapolis, IN. May 1992.

Treating Nicotine Addiction: A Challenge for the Recovery Professional. Vincent C. Pletcher, Linda S. Lysaght, and Vincent L. Hyman. Hazelden Foundation. Center City, MN. 1990.

Other Drugs

Hope, Faith & Courage: Stories from the Fellowship of Cocaine Anonymous. Cocaine Anonymous World Services, Inc. Los Angeles. 1993.

Narcotics Anonymous. World Service Office, Inc. Van Nuys, CA. 1984.

The New Drugs. Richard Seymour, M.S., David Smith, M.D., Darryl Inaba, Pharm. D., Mim Landry. Hazelden Foundation. Center City, MN. 1989. (Also may be ordered from Haight Ashbury Publications, 409 Clayton St., San Francisco, CA 94117.)

Violence

Love Does No Harm: Sexual Ethics for the Rest of Us. Marie M. Fortune. Continuum Publishing Group. New York. 1995.

Personal Safety Plan.[1] Sara M. Buel Esq. Special Counsel: Texas District & County Attorneys Association. Austin, TX. (512) 282-9688.

Trauma and Recovery: The Aftermath of Violence—from Domestic Abuse to Political Terror. Judith Lewis Herman, M.D. HarperCollins Basic Books. New York. 1992.

Women and Addiction

Many Roads, One Journey: Moving Beyond the Twelve Steps. Charlottte Davis Kasl, Ph.D. Harper Collins. New York. 1992.

Women and Drugs: Getting Hooked, Getting Clean. Emanuel Pelriso & Lucy Silvay Pelusa. CompCare Publishers. Minneapolis, MN. 1988.

Women and Addiction: A Collection of Papers. Stephanie S. Covington, Ph.D. La Jolla, CA. 1985.

---

1. A reliable, clear Personal Safety Plan is essential for the victim of violence. This plan is thoroughly tested, and is becoming a national model. Your local Police Department and Health Department may already have copies of it or you may request a copy from Sara M. Buel (512) 282-9688.

Catalogs

Some of the books, pamphlets, videos, and audio tapes in these catalogs also are available in Spanish.

Al-Anon Family Group Headquarters, Inc.—(800) 344-2666

Alcoholics Anonymous World Service, Inc.—(212) 870-3400

CENAPS—(800) 767-8181

CompCare Publishers—(800) 328-3330

Courage-to-Change—(800) 440-4003

Hazelden Foundation, Center City, MN—(800) 328-0098

U.S. Superintendent of Documents—(202) 512-1800

Videos

The preceeding catalogs also list videos.

Alcohol and the Family. Produced by AIMS Instructional Media Services. AIMS Multimedia, Distributor. Chatsworth, CA. 1985.

Alcoholism: Life Under the Influence. Nova series, produced by WGBH, Boston. 1984. (No longer distributed, but may be found in many libraries.)

Guidelines for Helping the Alcoholic. Fr. Joseph Martin. FMS Productions, Inc., Distributor. Carpenteria, CA. No. 1630 © 1976.

It Can Happen to Anyone. 1990. Check your library.

My Name Is Bill W. Featuring James Woods, James Garner. Hallmark Hall of Fame series. Produced and directed by Daniel Petrie. Warner Brothers. Burbank, CA. 1989.

Not in My Family: Parents' Experience of Adolescent Substance Abuse. Stephanie Ballmer, Psy.D. FMS Productions, Inc., Distributor. Carpenteria, CA. 1996.

Glossary

Addiction   A disease process characterized by the continued use of a specific psychoactive substance despite physical, psychological, or social harm.

ACA   These Adult Children of Alcoholics groups are part of Al-Anon.

ACOA   These Adult Children of Alcoholics groups are independent of Al-Anon.

Al-Anon   A self-help fellowship of families and friends of alcoholics.

Alcoholics Anonymous   A self-help fellowship whose sole purpose is to help alcoholics. In many parts of the country, AA also serves persons addicted to other drugs in addition to alcohol.

Alcoholism   A primary, chronic disease with genetic, psychosocial, and environmental factors influencing its development and manifestations. The disease is progressive and can be fatal. It is characterized by continuous or periodic impaired control over drinking, preoccupation with the drug alcohol, use of alcohol despite adverse consequences and distortions in thinking, most notably denial.[1]

Clean   Refers to an individual whose system is "clean" when tested for psychoactive drugs. Usually applies to street drugs.

Domestic Violence   Domestic violence is violence that occurs in private homes. It is a repetitive learned behavior. Its purpose is to establish and maintain power and control over another person. It may be one or a combination of verbal, emotional, physical, or sexual violence.

Dual Diagnosis   Two (sometimes more) coexisting primary diseases. As applied to addictive disease, dual diagnosis means the individual has addictive disease plus at least one other primary disease, which could be mental or physical or both.

Intervention   As applied to addictive disease, a specific method for interrupting the fatal progression of the disease by breaking

---

1. American Society of Addiction Medicine.

through the alcoholic/addict's denial system and convincing the person to seek recovery.

Polyaddiction Addition to more than one drug. Usually one drug is preferred (for example, alcohol, heroin, or a psychoactive prescription drug). Other psychoactive drugs are then often used to counteract undesirable effects of that drug.

Sober Refers to an individual who is abstinent from alcohol, but also extends to mean progressively improved behavior and attitudes, and a relatively balanced, serene life style.

Sponsor A clean and sober 12-step member who is asked by another member to be a guide and confidante in the recovery process. The sponsor does this by sharing personal experience, strength, and hope in order to promote another's healing. A sponsor is akin to a coach who supports and encourages an individual player. Sponsors do not function as professional counselors or therapists. The person being sponsored is usually called a "sponsee" or "pigeon."

12-Step Program A recovery program for persons with addictive disease based on the 12 Steps of Alcoholics Anonymous,[2] which are:

1. We admitted we were powerless over alcohol—that our lives had become unmanageable.
2. Came to believe that a Power greater than ourselves could restore us to sanity.
3. Made a decision to turn our will and our lives over to the care of God *as we understood Him.*
4. Made a searching and fearless moral inventory of ourselves.
5. Admitted to God, to ourselves, and to another human being the exact nature of our wrongs.
6. Were entirely ready to have God remove all these defects of character.

---

2. The Twelve Steps are reprinted with permission of Alcoholics Anonymous World Services, Inc. Permission to reprint The Twelve Steps does not mean that A.A. has reviewed or approved the contents of this publication, nor that A.A. agrees with the views expressed herein. A.A. is a program of recovery from alcoholism only—use of The Twelve Steps in connection with programs and activities which are patterned after A.A., but which address other problems, or in any other non-A.A. context, does not imply otherwise.

7. Humbly asked Him to remove our shortcomings.
8. Made a list of all persons we had harmed, and became willing to make amends to them all.
9. Made direct amends to such people wherever possible, except when to do so would injure them or others.
10. Continued to take personal inventory and when we were wrong promptly admitted it.
11. Sought through prayer and mediation to improve our conscious contact with God *as we understood Him,* praying only for knowledge of His will for us and the power to carry that out.
12. Having had a spiritual awakening as the result of these steps, we tried to carry this message to alcoholics, and to practice these principles in all our affairs.

"Working the Steps" The process of studying and applying the 12 steps to one's life. This is usually facilitated by association with others in a 12-step fellowship, including but not limited to one's sponsor. The steps need not be worked in any prescribed order nor in any required period of time. However, several of them tend to follow logically, and experience indicates that all the steps are typically addressed within the first two or three years by those who wish to remain or become clean and sober. Those with longer-term recovery usually find that recurrent attention to one step or another will be needed in order to maintain recovery.

NOTE: Other recovery programs such as those cited under Organizations (Rational Recovery, etc.) have each developed their own steps.[3]

---

3. The 12 Steps of Al-Anon are identical to AA's except for Step 12, which substitutes "we tried to carry this message to others" for "we tried to carry this message to alcoholics."

Other Books from Islewest

SEE WHAT I'M SAYING: What Children Tell Us Through Their Art
Dr. Myra Levick, Ph.D $15.95
Is your child in good emotional health? Struggling with a problem? Typical for his or her age? Dr. Levick says that the answers to all these questions can be seen in how and what your child draws. A leader in the field of Art Therapy, Levick gives expert help in understanding what children communicate through their drawings, and offers practical tools for assessing a child's intellectual and emotional development.

THROUGH THE INNER EYE: Awakening to the Creative Spirit
Jan Groenemann $19.95
Explore the expression of self as you are guided beyond self-imposed boundaries and reach within to your true self. Find more passion, purpose, and productivity in your life as you become free, creative, and whole.

RIGHT SIDE UP! Reflections for Those Living with Serious Illness
Marlene Halpin $10.95
The clarity and warmth of Ms. Halpin's poems and photos portray a sense of peace and well-being. One reflection per page makes this book manageable for those who are unable to focus for prolonged periods of time. **A Perfect Gift!**

HUNGER OF THE HEART: Communion at the Wall
Larry Powell $19.95
A powerful photo documentation of the healing impact that the Vietnam Veterans Memorial has on those who journey there. Powell offers a unique historical record of life at the Wall. His poignant photographs remind us that for thousands of suffering souls, their war is not over. *Hunger of the Heart* brings the healing power of the Wall to all those who are unable to personally visit the memorial.

THEY DO REMEMBER: A Story of Soul Survival
Sandy Robins 13.95
A story of survival, recovery, and hope for victims of abuse. This poignant autobiography will help abuse victims and survivors realize they do have a choice; they can choose to move from trauma to understanding and healing.

THE TOAD WITHIN: How to Control Eating Choices
Dr. James Weldon Worth $12.95
Dr. Worth's mythical creation, the Toad, is a metaphor for our appetite when it becomes difficult to control. By envisioning our runaway appetites as a mischievous and persistent Toad, who bullies us with food temptations, we have an adversary that can be visualized, confronted, and captured. Dr. Worth shows us how to engage in imaginary struggles with our Toad and defeat him or her by choosing wisely and courageously. Humorous and Insightful!!!

DOUBLE JEOPARDY: *Treating Juvenile Victims and Perpetrators for the Dual Disorder of Sexual Abuse and Substance Abuse*
Chris Frey, MSW, LCSW $36.95

Because it has become common for clients in treatment to present both childhood sexual abuse and substance abuse experiences, it is essential that helping professionals be well-versed in the dual disorder as they work to provide comprehensive recovery services. Double Jeopardy is a highly successful dual disorder treatment program that was originally developed for Boys Town of Missouri.

MEN AT WORK: *An Action Guide to Masculine Healing*
Chris Frey, MSW, LCSW

This book is written for men who want to heal their lives, men and women who want to better understand a loved one, and for therapists who are working with men. The book's approach has been designed to be utilized by the reader on his or her own, in therapy groups, and in self-help support groups.

BEYOND THE BLAME GAME: *Creating Compassion and Ending the Sex War in Your Life*
Dmitri Bilgere $10.95

Become a savvy CO (conscientious objector) in the war between the sexes. Dmitri Bilgere shows you how to stop unconsciously stimulating the behaviors you hate most in the opposite sex—and how to encourage behaviors you value. Learn how to untangle yourself from the blame game and **see your relationships improve instantly and permanently.**

THE PEACEFUL SOUL WITHIN: *Reflective Steps Toward Awareness*
Margot Robinson $14.95

The pain you suffer can make you a victim or a winner. Margot Robinson teaches you to **use the pain in your life as a means of transforming loss, failure, and even despair** into joyful self-acceptance and inner peace. Her down-to-earth reflections and practical exercises show you how to take control and responsibility for your own happiness.

SWALLOWED BY A SNAKE: *The Gift of the Masculine Side of Healing*
Thomas R. Golden $13.95

In clear, straight-forward terms, Golden **explains male grief and how it often goes unrecognized and unexpressed in traditional, verbal and emotional ways.** The masculine approach connects grief with action. Golden guides readers through the male experience of loss and shows how both men and women can benefit from understanding the masculine side of loss and healing.

THERE'S MORE TO QUITTING DRINKING THAN QUITTING DRINKING
Dr. Paul O $14.95

This book is **for recovering persons who know that abstinence is not recovery and who want more** than physical sobriety—who also seek mental, emotional, interpersonal, and spiritual sobriety. In an honest, humorous, heart-warming way, Dr. Paul shows how to develop new ways of thinking, feeling, communicating, and acting.

WALKING ON EGGSHELLS: When Someone You Care About Has Borderline Personality Disorder
Paul Mason, MS, and Randi Kreger   11.95

Coping with the behaviors of a BP—rage, extreme inconsistency, verbal abuse, impulsiveness, self-mutilation, and black-and-white thinking—can be devastating. Parents, spouses, lovers, friends, teachers—need answers NOW. *Walking on Eggshells* provides those answers quickly and clearly. This concise, 55 page booklet is loaded with information, strategies, examples, and support, designed to make sense of the BP's often incomprehensible behavior.

CREDIT, CASH, AND CO-DEPENDENCY
Yvonne kaye, PhD, MSC $15.95

Handling money can be troublesome—whether it's over-spending or under-spending (particularly for co-dependents and adult children of alcoholics).Yvonne Kaye, a counselor who specializes in co-dependency, Adult Child issues, and grief, knows that attitudes toward money are rooted in childhood. Speaking from experience, personal and professional, Dr. Kaye shows how to recognize the problems that surround compulsive spending or hoarding and shows how to work on recovery and develop happy, healthy monetary habits.

CAREGIVERS: REFLECTIONS ON COPING WITH CAREGIVING
Marlene Halpin, OP, PhD $14.95

"Intense caregivers feel increasingly isolated and depressed" concludes a new study from the National Family Caregivers Association. The study, "Caregiving Across the Life Cycle," reports that many intense caregivers suffer from depression accompanied by sleeplessness, isolation, and physical symptoms. Whether the one needing care is a parent, spouse, lover, child or a special friend—the demands must be fitted into an already full life. This book teaches caregivers how to find an acceptable balance between caring for others and caring for themselves.

HOPE FOR HEALING: Good News for Adult Children of Alcoholics
Rhea McDonnell, SSND and Rachel Callahan, CSC $9.95

There is a profound optimism in this books dynamic invitation to recovery. By identifying and explaining six basic steps, the authors provide many footholds for adult children who grew up in chemically dependent households on their healing journey. A guide to scaling the negative hurdles built through years of avoidance and denial.

WHOLING THE HEART: Good News for Those Who Grew Up in Troubled Families
Rea McDonnell, SSND and Rachel Callahan, CSC $10.95

Recognizing the ongoing effects of trouble in their family of origin, many adults today are seeking to heal the "holes" in their hearts caused by these early wounds. Grounded in the insights of both contemporary psychology and Scripture, this book, by offering suggestions for prayer and guided imagery, is a healing companion on that journey.

To Place a Credit Card Order Call
1–800–557–9867

Mention this ad for Free Shipping

Or send order and payment to: Islewest Publishing, 4242 Chavenelle Dr., Dubuque, IA 52002 Fax: 319–557–1376

Name _____

Address _____

City _____State _____Zip _____

Phone _____

Name of Book _____

Price: $ _____

Quantity _____

Shipping & Handling* $_____

Sales Tax (IA Residents 6%) _____

Total Enclosed $_____

Credit Card Information
❑Visa   ❑MasterCard

Credit Card # _____

Expiration Date _____

Signature _____

*$3.00 for first book
$.50 for each additional book

Call 1–800–557–9867 Now and Receive Free Shipping